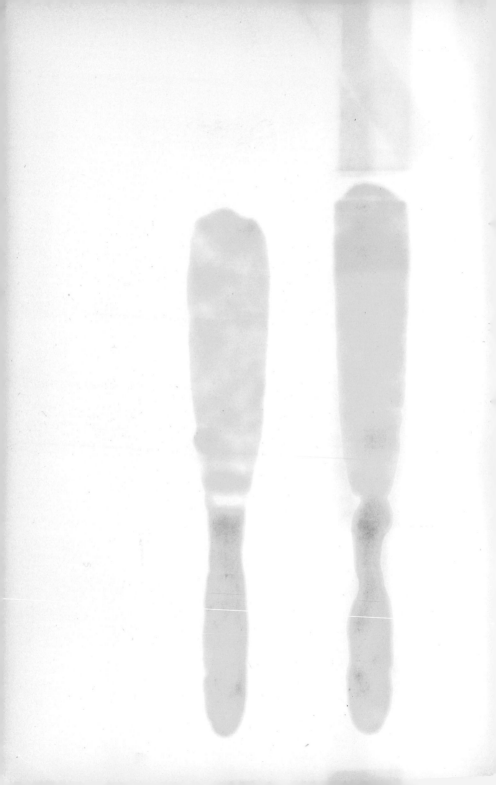

MAKING IT
THROUGH
MIDDLE AGE

WILLIAM ATTWOOD

———

MAKING IT THROUGH MIDDLE AGE

Notes While in Transit

ATHENEUM

NEW YORK

1982

Library of Congress Cataloging in Publication Data

[Attwood, William, 1919–
Making it through middle age.

1. Attwood, William, 1919– . 2. Middle age men—
United States—Biography. I. Title.
HQ799.95.A89 1982   305.2′4   81-69157
ISBN 0-689-11268-8   AACR2

Published simultaneously in Canada by McClelland and Stewart Ltd.
Manufactured by American Book–Stratford Press,
Saddle Brook, New Jersey
Designed by Harry Ford
First Printing April 1982
Second Printing July 1982
Third Printing September 1982

For Marty and Nathan

———

CONTENTS

1 INITIATION   3

2 CHOICES   17

3 SICKNESS   36

4 SEX   59

5 MARRIAGE   71

6 CHILDREN   84

7 GENERATIONS   102

8 WORK   115

9 COMMAND   130

10 RECOGNITION   149

11 SECURITY   164

12 RETIREMENT   181

13 DEATH   199

14 MEMORIES   212

15 CONTINUING   226

MAKING IT
THROUGH
MIDDLE AGE

I

INITIATION

IT CAN COME upon you suddenly and unexpectedly, like a toothache, or gradually, like low back pain. It's nothing to cheer about, or even look forward to, but as Mark Twain said of Wagner's music, "It's really not as bad as it sounds." The subject is middle age.

For me, the transition took place abruptly in February, 1964, in a farmhouse that once belonged to Isak Dinesen, the Danish writer, on the outskirts of Nairobi. The occasion was a diplomatic function, my first as the newly appointed American ambassador to Kenya, and I was greeted on arrival by a strikingly attractive young woman who introduced herself as a United States citizen and therefore "under your protection." Could she get me a drink? She could, and did.

After about ten minutes of what seemed like mildly flirtatious small talk, I decided that taking her out to dinner might be more entertaining than returning to the home of my temporary host, the embassy's economic attaché. I was forty-four and well married, and dinner, so help me, was all I had in mind. Then she asked, "Is your family here?"

I said my wife and three children would be joining me next month.

"Oh, I do hope you have a son my age! There's no one for me to date here."

So I had dinner with the economic attaché, feeling a good deal older and somewhat wiser; for the knowledge that you are no longer regarded as a contemporary by people with whom you feel contemporary is one of the first indications that you have crossed over to that graying area where most advertisers begin losing interest in your demographic profile.

The deep-down realization that life is finite and not renewable also comes with this territory, as does the knowledge that the orgiastic future in which Jay Gatsby believed will never come to pass, no matter how stubbornly you beat against the current.

A fortieth birthday party propels some people into middle age; others make the transition at fifty. A crippling illness can do it: in my case an attack of paralytic polio at forty-two only enraged me into fighting my way back to a slight limp, but a coronary at forty-eight was not the same; it triggered a clinical depression that left me outwardly intact but different, because fully aware—for the first time—of my own mortality. A marriage broken after many years can do it for some men, especially if followed by the usual liaison with a younger and more, well, energetic woman.

Whatever the catalyst, the thing happens some time after forty and can last into the seventies and even beyond, if your health and appearance hold up and nobody asks your age. It really ends only when you think of yourself as old and begin to act the part. Old age doesn't start with your first social security check; a person is the same at sixty-four as at sixty-five. But retirement might cause you to behave just differently enough for others to perceive you as "old."

The onset of middle age catches most of us unprepared, probably because of the emphasis and importance our culture places upon youth. Every marketing executive and television viewer knows that the years between eighteen and thirty-four ("the best sixteen years in a woman's life," according to a *Redbook* ad) are the desirable ones; after that, the wrinkles and the brown spots on the hands must be concealed like stigmata, and it's mostly arthritis, laxatives and dentures all the way to the retirement condo and the electric carts at Marina del Sol.

Not really, of course. The truth is that Americans between forty and seventy are 60 million strong and growing faster than any other demographic group—and that they are the people who really run things. They sell the products that the innocent eighteen-to thirty-four-year-old desirables spend their money on, they manage industry, dominate the government, control the universities and the media, and make most of the major decisions affecting the rest of the population. So be comforted, as you contemplate the misfortunes of middle age, by the fact that it remains the command generation.

The symptoms of middle age are as familiar and universal as the kind described in Ring Lardner's essay about reaching thirty-five: "The subject is woke up at 3 A.M.

by the fire whistle. He sniffles but can't smell no smoke. He thinks, well, it ain't our house and goes back to sleep."

When the subject reaches middle age he naturally wonders why Lardner didn't realize that thirty-five is *young*. There are other symptoms instantly recognizable to all of us who are riding on the down escalator: it gets late earlier—the idea of staying up past midnight becomes preposterous. Time also speeds up. February, which used to last about a year back in high school, now flashes by and suddenly it's spring, then summer again, and time for another birthday, which you hope people will forget.

What else? You no longer stay for the proffered nightcap at the end of the party. You walk into a room to get something and stand there, wondering what it could be. Most likely it's your glasses. When you read the paper you no longer skip the obit page: it's probable that someone you once met has died. You pick up a magazine, and the blurbs on the cover all sound silly—or irrelevant to your concerns. You wake up, and if it's after dawn, you are pleasantly surprised. You discover that almost everything that's fun to talk about happened at least twenty years ago. It takes much less time to get a satisfying physical workout. You avoid looking up old friends, not wanting to see the changes, especially if they're women. You find out the hard way that you are no longer particularly attractive to the opposite sex. And, when old girl friends call you, it's generally to ask for help and advice in finding a job for one of their kids.

Middle age is also a time when you must get used to having trouble—trouble getting really mad, or getting a different job, or getting an erection; trouble feeling a sense of anticipation about the future, or walking up a hill on a winter day, or having a really new experience—like doing something for the first time.

But these are for the most part surface symptoms, easy to get accustomed to, even to joke about. What happens internally is more interesting, and more heartening.

In middle age—if you have learned anything—it is possible to be more relaxed about a lot of matters that once seemed important, such as the impression you make on strangers or the impression they make on you; for our generation has, or should have, the assurance of having been tested and not found wanting. Self-consciousness, the bane of adolescence, evaporates—or should evaporate—by the time you're forty. To quote E. B. White on the subject: "Man staggers through life yapped at by his reason, pulled and shoved by his appetites, whispered to by his fears, beckoned by hopes. Small wonder that what he craves most is self-forgetting."

Immersing yourself in creative work or enlisting in a cause that seems momentarily to transcend self-interest are both well-beaten paths to this goal. And they do often make you come alive, a sensation for which you are ever more grateful the older you are if only because it is ever harder to achieve. Some of my contemporaries experienced it in the comradeship of World War II, our last popular crusade. Others found it in politics or sports. In my own case, I can remember a few brief shining moments in the early sixties while serving in what was called the New Frontier. When Jack Kennedy died I wrote a reminiscence that touched fleetingly on the shared enthusiasm of those thousand days: "Those of us who worked for him felt exhilarated and alive and prouder to be Americans than we'd ever been before. This is no small thing. It takes a lot to give you this kind of feeling when you're past forty and have, as they say, been around."

In between these all too infrequent highs, we begin to

understand in middle age that most of what we have been yearning for is probably unattainable and generally incommunicable. The apperception that so many of our contemporaries are still dreaming idealized and fanciful dreams in their middle years makes us more tolerant of—or indifferent to—their other shortcomings. For example, it's not easy for me today, at sixty-two, to identify with myself as the Princeton undergraduate who wrote editorials denouncing the socially stratified club system; or as the Stevenson speech writer incensed in 1956 by Nixon's artful innuendoes; or as the more recent magazine editor and newspaper publisher dismayed by the way mass communications can contribute to the diffusion of nonsense. And yet I can still understand the indignation I felt in these former roles, and can even share it now, in a muted fashion—muted because, as time goes by, we tend to become more tolerant, more . . . forbearing. Jonathan Swift wanted his epitaph to read that he had gone to a place "where fierce indignation can no longer tear my heart." Some of us get there before we die.

But if we care less strongly about most things, we care more deeply about those few things which the experiences of a lifetime have taught us are important: such as courage, humor, integrity and love.

I've been generalizing about my generation, knowing there are exceptions, as there are exceptions to everything. Not everyone glides into middle age, mellowing with the passing years. Some fight it, dyeing their hair or concealing their age. Some take up strenuous jogging, and some resume seducing young women, which can be even more strenuous, though easier on the knees and ankles. Others are momentarily enchanted by Dylan Thomas' lines: "Do not go gentle into that good night . . . / Rage, rage against the dying of the light." A few ignore the onset of decrepitude, or pretend to. But most of us in time make the adjustment, which really means distinguishing between what matters in life and what doesn't and then making the most of every increasingly precious year or month or day of relative health and vigor that we have left.

This book is one man's guide to the pleasures of these years. It is not a handbook on how to achieve happiness in middle age. (If you still think that happiness is an attainable state of existence, except fleetingly, then you are too young to be reading this book). All I'm offering, as the title suggests, are some pointers on making the best of it, although I believe that as much if not more enjoyment can be found at this time of our lives than in the overrated decades of our youth.

Look elsewhere if you are expecting a scholarly treatise or technical manual. You will find no footnotes or bibliography in this volume. My only source material is what I have learned and remember from six decades of highly eventful living, along with the corroborating testimony of a few close friends, all contemporary and anonymous. Because my research has been empirical—better yet, in French, *vécu*—not all my conclusions will apply or appeal to everybody. For instance, drawn as they are from a man's life, they may not all be relevant to women, although most of what I say will interest women who care about men. As for that splinter group of young fogies whose mentality becomes middle-aged at about twenty-five, they had better get off our tour bus right now if they have ridden this far.

What impels me to write this book? Why spend part of each day this fall, winter and spring facing a typewriter when I could be doing something less enervating. It isn't as though I had to prove to myself that I *can* write a book. I've written four—one on what it was like being a foreign correspondent in Europe in the forties; one on rediscovering America with my wife on a cross-country trip in the fifties; one on the adventure of serving as an ambassador to two African countries in the sixties; and a collection of scary stories for children. I also ghosted a book for a psychiatrist and collaborated on another about the sorry plight of American males. As an author friend in the agony of creation told me the other day, "It's a tough trade." Red Smith, the sports columnist, described it more vividly: "Writing a book isn't so hard. You just sit in front of a typewriter until little drops of blood appear on your forehead."

So why endure this self-inflicted torment? Well, there are two reasons for writing a book: either you need the money, or you need to say something. With me, it's more the story than the money. This is just as well, since the stuff of which six-figure best sellers are made—the kinky sex, the ruthless tycoons, the sadistic spies, the hopeless pill poppers, the gloomy mansions on the moors, the celebrity confessions, and the big bulky Kissinger-type things— just doesn't interest me. What does interest me is discovering something new and useful about the world and how to live in it, and then passing the information along in book form to other people. I often think of Mungo Park, the nineteenth-century Scottish explorer who was continually plunging into the unexplored wilds of Africa and then emerging at some estuary months later, usually on a stretcher, his companions decimated by malaria, his eyes sunken but ablaze with impatience to get back to the Royal Society or the Explorers' Club in London and relate all the wondrous things he had observed up and down the Congo or the Niger. I can identify with Mungo because there have been times in my life, as when I came home from an intensive care unit in 1967 or from China in 1971, when I've understood his need to communicate all that he had learned in what for him were undiscovered countries.

As a child, when asked by people what I wanted to be when I grew up, my answer was always, "an explorer." Now, looking back, I realize I have indeed done more exploring—sometimes by choice and sometimes by chance —of what life has to offer than my less restless contemporaries, most of whom set out from the start to find no more than a tolerable, secure, and enduring status quo. Today, when one of my acquaintances finds himself some place where I have already been, like a coronary care unit after a heart attack, I hurry over to tell him or her about my tennis game the day before and, oh, yes, not to worry about experiencing a probable but transient depression in a few weeks' time. In other words, when you've been there, the least you can do for others heading in that direction is to tell them what it's like, especially if the place seems kind of scary, like middle age.

So we can plan on covering a lot of ground in this book, especially since the material lends itself to detours and digressions. And I don't intend this journey to be boring for any of us. In fact, there's even a section on how to avoid boredom when there are fewer years, days and hours to waste.

On to the next question: what exactly are my credentials for being your self-appointed guide through the hills and dales of middle age? I'm not a gerontologist or a psychiatrist and have neither written nor read theses or monographs on the aging process. But I have done a good deal of field work.

For example, there's a chapter on choices—I've chosen to change jobs seven times since I was forty; there's one on sickness—I've had polio, a depression, two heart attacks, and a near-stroke since I was forty; three chapters deal with sex, marriage, and children—I was a young bachelor in Paris and New York in the forties and am now a thirty-one-year veteran of matrimony and the father of three children, two of whom were teenagers in the sixties, a coincidence which, as some of you know, qualifies me and my wife for special parental purple hearts; other chapters explore the work ethic and the executive world—I've been employed uninterruptedly in a variety of jobs, starting in Montreal as a reporter at fifteen dollars a week and ending as the president of a company with revenues of $140 million a year; and there's a chapter on fame—just for starters, I've traveled the celebrity circuit with the likes of Adlai Stevenson, Humphrey Bogart, Jackie Onassis, Earl Warren, Ginger Rogers, Judy Garland, Salvador Dali, Ingrid Bergman, Averell Harriman, the queen of England, and the queen of Greece; other chapters are concerned with security, memories, anxiety, and retirement—my father worked hard for his salary but never accumulated any money, so I'm familiar with having the monkey of apprehension on my back, but at sixty I retired from a high-paying job to do, among other things, some writing; other chapters touch on faith, loneliness, friendship and death—I've been alone in far places, watched friends confronting death, and myself seen its shadow just outside my door.

So much for credentials. What about my point of view? Is this going to be an upbeat sermon or a downbeat lecture?

A short answer is that one of my favorite philosophical quotations comes from Brendan Gill, the *New Yorker* critic and chronicler. "Not a shred of evidence exists," he once wrote, "in favor of the argument that life is serious, although it is often hard and even terrible." I would add that there are times when it's more fun *pretending* that certain things are serious—such as winning at games, increasing your company's sales, or outsmarting the other side in a diplomatic maneuver. And having fun is, after all, the most serious business of life, as all children instinctively know but then forget when they reach adolescence.

My own philosophy is that the purpose of life is to enjoy it. This is not as hedonistic as it sounds. If God indeed exists, I believe He, She, or It would cheer us on for trying to make the most of our lifetime sentence on earth. Also, very few people find lasting enjoyment in self-indulgence; most of us, consciously or not, are more likely to subscribe to the ancient Greeks' definition of happiness that Jack Kennedy was so fond of citing: the exercise of vital powers in the direction of excellence in a life affording them scope. In plainer English—working at what you can do best.

So I suppose you could describe my point of view as guardedly optimistic about the human condition and the years I have left to live. I'm just as glad they aren't going to spill over into the twenty-first century, when today's problems are more likely to be magnified than ameliorated. Overpopulation, endemic poverty, and spreading pollution won't be effectively dealt with by the tribes of man as presently constituted into disputatious nation-states. Up until recently, things have been getting both better *and* worse; for example, advances in medicine have eliminated a lot of painful and disabling ailments, while the urbanization and depersonalization of societies have produced a new and growing class of people all over the world whose lives have neither structure nor roots. But now, as we drift toward the year 2000, it may take a disaster of universal proportions, like a global famine or the fallout from a few devastating nuclear explosions, to shock the next generation into realizing that the changes wrought by science and technology, while far-reaching and irreversible, are manageable only if we disenthrall ourselves from obsolete concepts, like gunboat diplomacy. And that's another advantage of being middle-aged in the 1980s: we can do our part to help the next generation take action now to avert disaster, but we won't be here to suffer the consequences if it louses things up.

So I'm an optimist, even if guardedly; concerned, still, about the world as it will be after my leaving it; and a long, long way from the celebrated essayist, Joan Didion, who, in *The White Album*, introduced herself to her readers as follows:

> I want you to know, as you read me, precisely who I am and where I am and what is on my mind. I want you to understand exactly what you are getting: You are getting a woman who for some time now has felt radically separated from most of the ideas that seem to interest other people. You are getting a woman who somewhere along the line misplaced whatever slight faith she had in the social contract, in the meliorative principle, in the whole grand pattern of human behavior. Quite often during the past several years I have felt myself a sleepwalker, moving through the world unconscious of the moment's high issues, oblivious to its data, alert only to the stuff of bad dreams. . . .

No, I am not Joan Didion, nor would want to be. You are getting someone else in this album. All of us can have some pretty bad dreams after forty, but some of us are alert to much more. This is not to say that the years covered in this book are golden ones—far from it. But they have contained enough poignantly bright moments for me to wish they might be prolonged: weekends at Molo, in the Kenyan highlands, galloping on horseback through the coffee plantations with my kids, Peter and Jan, the fragrance of woodsmoke in the thin, cool evening air; deep-sea fishing with my wife, Sim, far out in the tropical Atlantic, then camping out on one of the palm-fringed islands cooking our catch and watching the sunset-colored water; candlelit evenings in Georgetown gardens during the vibrant comradeship of the New Frontier; coming home from an overseas assignment, relaxed in the plane, knowing I had a good story and looking forward to writing it; tucked in the stern of a canoe with my youngest daughter, Suzy, as we skimmed along the surface of a placid lake at sundown in the wilderness of northern Lapland. . . .

I don't know for certain which are the best years of our lives; I suspect they vary from person to person. But I do know that each decade of mine has been an improvement over the one before, although I'm not deep enough into my seventh to make a judgment yet about this one. At sixty, it dawns on you that no matter how young you feel in body and spirit, you are considered to be old, at least by strangers. Reading a story in the *New York Times* the other day, I came across the phrase "two elderly women" and noticed that one was just my age.

At this moment, my thoughts are turned to some things I'll be doing in the year ahead, and, so help me, I don't feel much different from the way I did five or ten years ago; but there's no escaping the two numerals—not to mention the statistics—that identify me as a senior citizen.

Of course, I haven't yet reached that sobering milestone where, if you get a new dog, you can be reasonably sure it will outlive you. Looking at my aging, asthmatic Yorkshire terrier, I think the odds are that he'll get to the big kennel in the sky first. But as for his successor. . . .

Yet I feel good today. This morning I took my grandson, Nathan, to his first swimming class, reflecting that it was just twelve years since I took Suzy to the same place for *her* first lesson, when her sister, Jan, was the instructress. As I delivered him to the new teacher, she told him, "Say good-bye to your daddy."

"That's not my daddy," he replied scornfully, "that's my *grandpa!*"

And then he gave me a big hug.

Well, the walk back up the hill was a little more strenuous than twelve years ago, but I didn't notice it, nor feel a backache from yesterday's exercise nor the headache from last night's wine. The music of "That's my *grandpa!*" was all that mattered.

Oh, to make it all last just a little longer!

But these are the most fleeting years of all, just when you have finally got the terrain figured out and still have the stamina, along with the experience, to scale a few more peaks and tolerate the valleys and avoid the dismal swamps.

Do you still want to see what the landscape of middle age looks like from where I am today? Here goes.

2

CHOICES

I SHOULD TELL YOU that this chapter, like certain others to follow, is not for everybody who is immersed in or contemplating middle age. It is for those who know that life's three essential and strongest drives are for security, for identity, and for stimulation, and who sense that the last—or perhaps the last two—may be missing from theirs. It is for those who perceive themselves as trapped in routines gone stale and who can feel the cement hardening around their ankles. And it's to encourage would-be explorers of life's uncharted areas not always to take the easier path when they come to a crossroad, and, when faced with a choice, to make a conscious decision.

I've made several life-changing decisions in my time—

some of the biggest ones since I was forty. And I have found out that it's never too late—not up to now anyway—to start out on a new tack. In fact it can be easier, in some ways, as you get older because of the freedom of action that comes with a network of friends, a variety of acquired skills, and children finally grown and gone.

This chapter, in short, is about recognizing opportunities as they float by; when and why to seize them, and how the consequences can give flavor and meaning to these years that nobody looks forward to. Not all of us are born with a restless streak, or an unquenchable curiosity about all that life has to offer; not all of us reach middle age haunted by remorse about how we've spent—or misspent—the years behind and resolved to salvage some few good moments before the lights go out. The truth is that a great many people are more or less satisfied with things as they are—satisfied enough so that they are not about to risk whatever status and security they have achieved in order to explore some unfamiliar byway or bayou. There are the young fogeys whom I advised in the last chapter to quit this trip before we go any further. There are those who would just as soon drift with the tide, going to work and back, watching television, making love to their wives once a week, taking major league sports seriously, fishing and hunting boisterously in season, sleeping soundly every night. There are those who like to stay put, in the town where they grew up or with the company that first hired them, and are content to move deliberately, if not always far, up the executive staircase. Finally, there are those who evince no desire to explore beyond, perhaps, the tidy charms of a new holiday resort, the accessible favors of a neighbor's wife or husband or the fairways of an exclusive golf course.

Yet I have often been surprised (but not anymore), by

how many professedly contented people will tell you late at night and after many drinks, how much they want to get away from moribund marriages and boring jobs, how often they wish they had ranged more widely—the men usually on sailboats in the tropics, the women usually on balconies in Rome or Paris. Sudden, unexpected divorces a few months later are reminders that much of this late-night talk springs from a deeper source than eighty-six-proof vodka.

There are also those who can't—can't strike out, or don't think they can, which comes to the same thing. My father had no latitude for choice back in 1933, lucky just to have a job. He could have walked away. I knew some fathers who did then, but most didn't. And he didn't; he just got drunk once a month. Today, while there's no depression, I have friends who have been "buying colleges" for years for a succession of not always appreciative children. They too are, in effect, trapped if they choose to be dutiful parents. Women, until fairly recently, have been denied many choices, even the choice of how many children they want to have.

And there are those who hesitate. How can they be sure that a decision affecting where and how they live will be right or wrong? They can't, of course. But they should heed the words of Roy Lyman Wilbur, the former president of Stanford University, who once said, "I have many decisions to make, and some of them are wrong. But I have learned that there is something worse than a few wrong decisions, and that is indecision."

Be thankful, then, if you feel free enough to make decisions. Most people are too boxed in to consider alternatives. Others are like an old friend of mine who always thought that what he wanted was money so that he could get out of the box. He finally made the money and is still in the box. Why? Because, while he can now lift the lid, he doesn't know what he wants to do if he does. He's been there too long: never having made choices, he lost the knack.

So you make the wrong decision; you take the fork in the road that becomes a detour. What of it? You can always head for the interstate and try again, knowing of course that you have forfeited the choice of the *other* fork. But there will always be more forks as you go along; better ones, if you are on the lookout and put to good use the topographical knowledge you've acquired from making wrong turns.

One final word before we buttress these generalities with some empirical evidence: making choices or decisions is a habit, like smoking or not smoking; and, as with most habits, it is acquired early and easily, generally in the teens, although it is possible, with more exertion, to learn the habit in later life.

I mentioned integrity in the last chapter as being one of the few things left in the sieve after you have shaken out most of a lifetime's accumulation of trash. At Princeton, where I spent four years, there was and still is something called the honor system. It means that exams are unsupervised, and students are free to come and go as they please. Whether or not to cheat by looking up an answer is a student's own decision, and the system works pretty well, or did then.

In my senior year I discovered that in order to graduate I had to pass an elective course in Italian Renaissance painting which I had chosen because I found it restful, three days a week after lunch, to sit in a darkened room looking (or not looking) at a series of color slides projected on a screen. Now, faced with an exam, I located a

tutor and some Dexedrine tablets and spent the night before the exam making sure I could remember that Giotto's
Christs were chubby and Botticelli's Madonnas looked
anemic. But in the morning I found that the exam also
called for an analytical essay about Ghirlandaio, a painter
whose slides I had missed in the darkness. So I walked out
and sat on the steps of the sundial that is an old campus
landmark, and smoked a cigarette. I looked at the library
a couple of hundred yards away and thought how easy
it would be to stroll over there and come back with
enough information to write a passable essay. I even got
up and began walking. Then I paused, sat down again
and lit another cigarette; and finally returned to the exam
and put some words together about the artist—fortunately
much of what can be said about Italian Renaissance
painters is readily interchangable—and emerged from the
course with a marginal but passing grade.

I remember the sundial forty years later because it was
one of those moments when you make a seemingly small
choice that will affect many others in the course of your
life, choices which can either build the kind of psychic
muscle we all need or leave you weaker and less and less
pleased with your own company—which is a miserable
way to live.

How does one choice affect another? Seven years after
the sundial, as a *New York Herald Tribune* reporter, I
happened to be passing through Warsaw, where I heard
rumors of serious rioting in Cracow, eight hours away by
train. It would have been easy to concoct a printable
story; I even knew the cliché lead of those days to use
under a Cracow dateline: "Red terror gripped this city
tonight as grim-faced tommy-gunners patrolled the rubble-
strewn streets." But I'd have been faking it. I thought again

of the sundial, as I often had in the intervening years, and took the lousy—literally lousy—train to Cracow and got the story right: there weren't any riots to report.

All these choices in time do develop that muscle I call psychic rather than moral because it has to do mainly with knowing who you are and then having the strength to be true to that self. They say that nice guys finish last. I'm not sure about that. What I do know is that tough guys finish first—and that toughness is not necessarily composed of brawn or brilliance or ambition. Toughness is what comes from thinking things out at sundials and other places and getting your priorities sorted out so that by midlife that knack of making decisive choices has become a deeply ingrained habit, and the ability to make wise ones well developed.

Some of the choices made during a lifetime may not always seem wise in retrospect. But if the choice feels right at the time, then it is always better to make it, even if the consequences are disappointing. Two wartime examples may illustrate the point. In the fall of 1941 I could have become a combat correspondent instead of a soldier, but journalism, that particular December, did not seem to be where the action was. I was wrong, as it turned out. My impulsive choice led to four years of somewhat aimless training and travel at government expense from the Middle East to the Western Pacific, all of it aggravated by the frustration of knowing I was not making the slightest contribution to the war effort. But the choice, the decision to enlist when I did, is not something I regret, because it was the natural action for me to take just then.

My other example is somewhat more vivid and certainly unique. In the fall of 1943, just out of Officers' Candidate School at Fort Sill, Oklahoma, I was ordered to Washington for assignment to something called Special Branch,

Military Intelligence Service. It sounded adventurous, but, as I found out early in 1944 in London, it was a safe but dull desk job connected with the secret British code-cracking operation known as Ultra.

One night, in the pub of a village called Leighton Buzzard, it dawned on me that I was the wrong man, at twenty-four, for this kind of duty. In the morning I asked our commanding officer for a transfer out, anywhere. Something was driving me toward combat or at least toward hardship and danger, probably because I needed, then, to find out how I would react to them.

So I made my stubborn choice, and I paid a price. The trail I chose to take one winter night in Leighton Buzzard ended more than a year later with an explosion on a hill on Okinawa. In between I learned to overcome my fear of high places in parachute school with the 13th Airborne Division; learned to beach a rubber boat in surf with the 97th Infantry Division; learned some geography in the Pacific, from Hawaii to New Guinea to Leyte and then on, with the 7th Infantry Division, to Okinawa, an island redolent in the spring of 1945 with the sweet, sickening stench of crushed sugar cane and death. It was here that I finally found the answer to the question that had nagged me in England, the question about how I would react to danger, to being under fire. I might have known what it would be: like everybody else, I was scared shitless.

About the explosion, and then we'll wrap it up and move along. By June 21, 1945, all that the Japanese held on Okinawa was a hill laced with caves on the southern tip of the island. I was told by our colonel to take a squad of the recon troop, locate the Japanese general's command post, and come back with his sword before some other unit, especially the marines, found it first. We were hardly a gung-ho group: nobody wanted to get shot up at that point in the war just for a trophy, so we made our way very gingerly to the crest of the hill. Then came the big bang, as the last Japanese mortar lobbed its last round a few yards in front of us. Some of us were knocked down by the blast, but no one was hit badly except a Canadian liaison officer who caught some fragments in his chest. We picked him up and, expecting a banzai charge, fled like rabbits. Thus, the last engagement between United States and Japanese ground forces in World War II ended in a headlong American retreat. As for the sword, a naval officer, strolling along the cliffs the next day, found the general's body impaled upon it, hara-kiri style, on a ledge overlooking the sea.

But what the hell. I was home a few months later, after Hiroshima, with a better trophy, a sword of my own from a Japanese officer I'd captured; and then in December, four years to the day after enlisting, I was free at last.

Looking back across the decades, was the choice I made in 1944 right or wrong? Right, I think, because the choice was triggered by a strong impulse, and right because I traveled the distance with the consequences. I was lucky, too, to have escaped with so few bruises.

I warned you we'd occasionally be disgressing, or seeming to.

Now back to the main theme, which is making choices in middle age. First off, remember that any life-altering choice can *seem* harder to carry out after you're forty, though it's really not. I can think offhand of six women friends, including my wife, who successfully embarked on careers in their forties—in part because they needed identities not linked to their married names and in part because, with the children gone, they also required more stimulation than could be found at bridge tables, tennis courts, or the League of Women Voters. In some cases, the added income was a secondary factor. My wife and a friend chose to sell real estate, another friend went to law school and is now a practicing attorney, another got a master's degree and became a teacher, a former actress turned to directing and a onetime researcher became assistant to the president of a large corporation. Only one has been divorced, and the action was unrelated to her choosing to start a full-time, midlife career. In fact, I'd guess that all of them now get along better with their husbands than other wives who have drifted in and out of their forties without ever making a self-affirming move.

We've been talking about getting the habit of making a decision when presented with a choice. But what do you do when it's clear that, while no choice is yet apparent, the urge to change your way of life is stronger than inertia, stronger than your normal inclination to suppress it? Let's go back in time again, to the summer of 1959, the year I turned forty.

"Togetherness" was a buzz word of the fifties and the theme of much magazine marketing of that time. I can still see Mom and Dad and the two kids—the girl about nine and her brother a shade younger and shorter—heading for a family outing in the two-toned station wagon with giant fins. The boy wears a Davy Crockett coonskin hat and carries a baseball bat; his sister has the beach ball and her hula hoop; Mom, impeccably coiffed and earrings in place, has the picnic hamper, Dad the fishing poles or his golf clubs—and all are smiling, even the spaniel, barking joyously as he races ahead across the well-tended lawn. There's a white colonial split-level with green shutters in the background. Why shouldn't they smile? Dad is clearly the kind of upwardly mobile suburban executive for whom the Edsel was designed, the sun is always shining, the kids are never surly, and everybody likes Ike.

With a few variations, I could almost see myself and my family in this picture. Peter was eight and Jan seven, our dog was a poodle who understood only French, our house was a flat-roofed contemporary, and we preferred Adlai to Ike. But five days a week, briefcase in hand, I took the 8:04 A.M. train to New York and the 5:34 P.M. back; on weekends I did chores, played bridge, went to crowded parties, and skated or hit tennis balls in season. I was making more than $20,000 a year—good money in those days—doing interesting, creative work as foreign editor of *Look*. The big general magazines were still in their heyday and I traveled a lot—often with Sim—to India to see Nehru, Egypt to see Nasser, Israel to see Ben Gurion, and Cuba to see Hemingway.

In short, we had a good life in 1959, by almost any measurement. So why did I feel restless and vaguely dissatisfied? Was it the prospect, at forty, of riding the commuter train for another quarter century while I slowly climbed the *Look* ladder, maybe all the way to the editorship? I recall the phrase in Charles Jackson's book, *The Lost Weekend:* "The barometer of his emotional nature was set for a spell of riot." My barometer was set for a season of change. The year before I had heard about the symptoms from Ingrid Bergman, in London where she was making a movie. We'd been friends ever since *Look* had done a sympathetic story about her in 1952, when she was condemned and ostracized back home for leaving her husband to live in Italy with the director, Roberto Rosselini. Now, having left Rosselini and about to marry an old Swedish friend, she spoke of the past: "One day I was sitting by my swimming pool in Beverly Hills. I had two wonderful children and a loving husband and I was a big Hollywood star. And then I noticed the tears were running down my cheeks." Soon afterward she happened to see a Rosselini picture, wrote him a letter offering to act in his next film, and within a few months joined him in Stromboli.

I was no star in 1959, not even a bad actor, and I didn't own a pool and would have had a hard time crying. But I knew how Ingrid had felt, a few years short of forty. And at such moments in life, something often happens—a picture show, a chance encounter, an opportunity knocking. But you have to be alert to the sound, and be able to recognize it, and then get to the door quickly before it goes away, because, as the cliché says, the same opportunity doesn't knock twice.

My opportunity to make a move came in December of 1959, on a flight between Washington and New York. My seatmate was Adlai Stevenson, with whom I'd traveled around the world six years earlier. He'd been thinking about the 1960 campaign and the importance of defeating Nixon, whom he detested, and wanted to have some speeches ready on the chance that a deadlocked convention would again turn to him. Would I be willing to take a leave of absence and help out, if the money were made available to match my salary? I told him I'd have to talk to Sim and think it over. But, feeling just as he did about Nixon, I knew what my decision would be, whether or not *Look* granted me a leave. The needle of my emotional barometer was fixed on change.

The decision made that winter (the matching money was found, the leave granted) led to a series of choices over the next few years that are worth recounting briefly because they all occurred in my forties, that decade generally regarded as the first and most traumatic of middle age. This is when your options are supposed to dry up, along with your desire to pursue them. It's not so. Not *necessarily* so.

In the spring of 1960 I met more politicians and wrote more speeches than I had in a lifetime. Stevenson was reluctant either to challenge Kennedy or to endorse him, so the convention in July, though noisy, lacked suspense; the galleries yelled for Adlai but the delegates voted for Jack. Earlier, Kennedy had invited me to join his speech-writing staff for the fall campaign, and so in August I was in Washington, helping to stockpile the words that would be the ammunition of the next two months. (One example: "I don't want America to be first—*if,* first—*but,* or first—*when.* I want America to be first—*period.*")

With one or two exceptions, like the crucial address to the Protestant ministers in Houston, Kennedy didn't attach much importance to speeches. "By October," he told us one evening, "all that will matter is which candidate the people feel they can trust." And he saw the difference between himself and Nixon as being more temperamental than ideological: "Nixon just wants to be president. I want to be president because I plan to use the power of the office to get things done."

It was soon obvious that Stevenson's more ideological and still faithful legions were not flocking to Kennedy, and in mid-September I was assigned to join Stevenson on a cross-country speaking tour to stir up his followers. They had to hear it from him that Kennedy was a real liberal. And hear it they did, at more than seventy rallies in the next five weeks. But it was a difficult role for him to campaign for somebody else after twice being the candidate. One night in Sacramento, after delivering a blistering, crowd-pleasing attack on Nixon, he was met outside by a crowd of reporters. "Hey, governor," somebody called out, "how do you like being Jack Kennedy's hatchet man?" Stevenson winced and told me later he would never use that speech again.

Came November and that long, long election night, and suddenly I was back on the 8:04 A.M. train and in my old office, feeling even more restless than before my excursion into politics. It's been said that journalism gives you the best chance of being a part of the history of your own time. That's true, if you are satisfied to be an observer of events, but in 1960 I had been a participant of sorts and had enjoyed it. So when Stevenson was named ambassador to the United Nations and asked me to be his public affairs officer, I thought about it seriously before deciding that my *Look* job offered more variety as well as money.

Then Chester Bowles, who'd been appointed undersecretary of state, asked me for some names of people who might want to come into the State Department. Before leaving for a Caribbean vacation in December I sent him some and added, as a casual afterthought, "If you ever need an ambassador to Guinea, I'd like a chance to apply."

We came home January 9. Bowles called that evening while Sim was ironing and I was watching the snow fall and wondering if the trains would be running in the morning. He talked about a foreign policy article I was writing and then said, "By the way, I think you're all set for Guinea." When he hung up I said to Sim, "I'll be damned. We're going to Africa." She looked up from her ironing and said, "Fine. When do I start packing?" And that's how easy it was to make the second big choice of my forties decade.

The next came in 1963, after we'd been in Guinea more than two years. I asked to come home, both for professional reasons (my job was done, the Soviet thrust there blunted) and personal considerations (the climate was debilitating and there was no school for the kids.) Back in Washington, on the eve of my forty-fourth birthday, I had another decision to make: whether to stay in government—and if so, where; or to go back to *Look*, where Dan Mich, the editor, wanted me to succeed him on his retirement; or to accept an offer to be a television news executive.

I chose the New Frontier, an exciting place to be at that time in history; also, old friends at the State Department and in the White House hinted at interesting assignments in the offing. But after a couple of weeks of reading items in the *New York Times* and the *Washington Post* naming me as the probable next ambassador to, successively, Yugoslavia, Chile, Mexico, Indonesia and Argentina, I began to feel like an unemployed actor (with a good press agent) for whom no part can be found. Offers did come up—from Ed Murrow at USIS and from Roswell Gilpatric at the Pentagon—but living in Washington, a federal company town, didn't appeal to Sim or me.

Finally, with my home leave and my monthly paycheck about to run out, I met the president at a party at the home of Joe Alsop, the columnist. He suggested I drop in and talk about my future plans. I told him I'd had a request for an appointment pending for ten days. Well, the thing to do, he said, was just to call his secretary, Mrs. Lincoln. So I did, and saw him the next day in the oval office. After talking for ten minutes about a woman we'd both known since prep school, we spent five minutes on my future. He said Latin America was important, and the ambassadorship to Colombia would be open in December. Meanwhile I could be an advisor on African affairs to the United States mission to the United Nations, if Stevenson was agreeable. He was, and that was that.

So Sim and I brushed up on our Spanish that summer

and fall, and the United Nations proved to be more interesting than I'd anticipated after I got involved in some confidential negotiations with the Cubans about normalizing relations. Then came the assassination, and after the shock waves had subsided, a call came from Wayne Fredericks, then deputy assistant secretary for African affairs. President Johnson, he said, wanted as many of us who had served in Africa under Kennedy to go back, to demonstrate continuity. Would I be interested in going to Kenya, now on the verge of independence? It sounded right: the job would be challenging enough, with Jomo Kenyatta, the alleged old Mau-Mau leader, about to take over; the climate was healthful—we were expecting a new baby; and there were British schools in Nairobi for the kids. I got Sim's okay and was sworn in the next month. Another opportunity, another choice, another decision—and it was only four years since my talk with Stevenson on the plane to Washington. It was getting easier every time.

The more than two years we spent in Kenya were among the best Sim and I have known. I wrote a book about them and the Guinea years, called *The Reds and the Blacks*. But by the spring of 1966, the old time-for-a-change feeling recurred. United States–Kenya relations were off to a good start, despite some rough moments, like the Stanleyville rescue operation; the two older children needed better schools than existed in Kenya—and a less rootless existence; and at forty-six, I had to decide whether to say in government or return to journalism before the attractive options were foreclosed. My inclination was to get out. Already it was harder to defend publicly our involvement in Vietnam, and I knew that if the Republicans won the White House—as they did in 1968—I'd be out of a job anyway. That's why a visit to Kenya by my former boss, Mike Cowles, came at an opportune time. He

wanted an editor-in-chief for his new communications conglomerate, of which *Look* was a part, and I certainly
would be needing a congenial and remunerative job back
home. Once again, with middle age closing in fast, Sim
and I had chosen change.

The years at Cowles Communications were neither the
best nor the worst of my working life. But by 1970 I saw
handwriting on the wall that read like an epitaph for general magazines. Moreover, the effort to protect *Look*'s
editorial integrity from the pressures of a desperate advertising department was becoming a biweekly strain. So I
made up my mind to leave by the end of the year and
embark on a less structured life. I began quietly talking
to publishers about doing books and to friends at the networks about the possibilities of adapting the general magazine format to television. My emotional barometer, at
fifty-one, was once again pointing to change.

In late August the phone rang. It was Otis Chandler,
publisher of the *Los Angeles Times,* whom I'd heard of
but never met. His company, Times Mirror, had bought
Newsday, the Long Island daily, in May, and had been
looking for a publisher ever since. He suggested I fly out
to the West Coast and talk about it. The timing was just
right. In his office we didn't waste words: I wanted no
contract, and he had none to offer me. I told him my
strengths—news judgment, public relations, and motivating people—and my weaknesses—finance and production.
But I knew enough about profit and loss to understand
that increasing revenues or lowering costs—or better yet,
doing both without sacrificing quality—was always the
objective. Most of the rest was jargon. Finally, having
agreed on terms and salary he suggested we see his father,
Norman Chandler—courtly, venerated, a pillar of California's Republican establishment.

"What are your politics?" he asked.

"I'm a registered Democrat."

"Are you interested in this job?"

"I wouldn't have come out here if I weren't."

"Welcome aboard."

The *Newsday* job appealed to me because I had discovered in government that I liked running things. The paper enjoyed complete editorial autonomy, although corporate financial controls were strict from the start, and, paradoxically, grew stricter the more profitable the paper became. So I stayed there nearly nine years as president, publisher and chairman, the longest I'd stayed in any job—and the longest, I think, most people are able to hold a chief executive's position without getting somewhat stale. The things for which I was hired and held responsible were accomplished—the Sunday paper launched, the various departments integrated, the profits sextupled, the management team restructured, the latest technology phased in, the new $40-million plant completed. It was time to move on, at sixty, while I still had some fuel in my tank, a few still unfulfilled ambitions, and enough money to indulge my curiosity about places not yet explored or emotions not yet experienced.

Most people would say I've been very lucky. But luck in life is not like luck at the roulette table. You have to prepare for it. "A lazy man," says a Persian proverb, "is never lucky." Stephen Leacock said it a little differently: "I am a great believer in luck, and I find that the harder I work the more I have of it." If you work hard and move around and acquire new skills and leave friends and not enemies behind when you change jobs, then your prospects for having interesting options in middle age are enhanced.

Mobility is also a factor in multiplying your range of

choices. Every time you change jobs you meet new people, learn new things and see new sights. Certainly every change I chose to make in life—from college to army to a newspaper to freelancing to a magazine to politics to diplomacy to corporate communications to publishing and to my present eclectic life style has been aided by the people I met and the knowledge I acquired at each stage along the way. And with mobility you develop the self-confidence that comes from coping with unfamiliar situations and discovering unsuspected talents within yourself. You learn that a new job is seldom as hard as it seems once you've mastered the vernacular that goes with it, and that resigning from one you don't like—as in dissolving an unhappy marriage—can be a liberating experience. Your readiness to resign can also be a source of strength with employers who assume that everybody is insecure, everybody can be pushed around, and everybody has his or her price.

And it certainly helps, if you plan on moving around in life, to have a supportive and adaptable marriage partner, as I have; one who agrees that making a move is almost always exhilarating and rejuvenating.

One final word: in middle age, you are usually in a better position to take charge of your life than at any other time. This is when you are most likely to have the skills and confidence that help widen your range of options. But this is also the time when good health can no longer be taken for granted. Illness, the topic of the next chapter, can certainly limit the options—though serious illness need not impair your ability to function, to work, or to have fun, even if it cripples a part of your body. In middle age, it's nice but not all that important to run, or even to walk fast in order to lead a full life. And it's possible to adjust to all kinds of ailments that once seemed devastating. So if it's a matter of just restricting your choices, well, that's all right. But it's different if you allow a serious illness to ground you psychologically as well as physically. I've seen too many of my contemporaries come out of hospitals like burnt-out cases—strangely placid, as if the mere act of waiting to die were reason enough to go on living. And that's not all right.

3

SICKNESS

WE SAY somebody's "in the hospital." The British say "in hospital." I prefer their phrase. It sounds more like "in extremis" or "in limbo" or just "in trouble," all of which we ex-patients can readily associate with the places ambulances have taken us.

Most people manage to escape prolonged hospitalization—as I did, except for a bout with hepatitis—until they've crossed the forty-year threshold. But in middle age it's reasonable to expect that you'll be seeing more of hospitals and doctors' offices than ever before. Your body, like a car with 100,000 or more miles on the clock, inevitably requires more maintenance. Therefore a chapter on coping with sickness—both the major illnesses and the everyday ailments—not only belongs in this book, it belongs up front.

Serious sickness other than cancer is usually of short duration and really unpleasant only in its early stages. The pain of a heart attack, for instance, seldom lasts more than a half hour; after that the chances are that you are either dead or on the mend, so don't expect this chapter to be depressing. It may in fact cheer you up, as it did me, to learn that hardly anybody feels as fine as they pretend to; and that getting really sick, and then recovering, can actually broaden and improve your outlook on life and enhance your enjoyment of it. And if that sounds like Pollyanna, so be it.

First let's note and dispose of these everyday ailments that are as much a part of our middle years as pimples and athlete's foot were a part of our teens.

I mean "everyday" quite literally. For these are the years when no one feels really well for any length of time. There are moments, of course, when a sense of physical well-being washes over you; for example after a restful afternoon nap followed by some moderate exercise—perhaps a walk and a swim—and a couple of drinks at sunset. But these moments are rare. Ask one of us, "How are you?" and notice how often we hesitate before saying, "Fine!" or even, "Okay." We are all momentarily tempted to be honest and give a more clinically accurate answer. "How did you sleep?" asks the occasionally solicitous spouse from his or her side of the bed. "Not too badly," is the most positive reply the spouse can expect. It's a rare morning among my contemporaries when anyone wakes up fully rested, let alone bushy-tailed.

This is also a time when you can no longer do some things without paying a heavy and even unacceptable price. You don't go horseback riding, as I did in Scotland with my daughter, and then try to play golf the next day, let alone bend over to pick up the ball. ("That fookin' horse fooked up your game, sir," said my sympathetic caddy.)

Backs act up; so do knees, necks and elbows. Indigestion, hemorrhoids, skin rashes, arthritic aches, and mysterious muscular twinges come and go and come again. You get to know your dentist and ophthalmologist a lot better. You strain to hear the things that people seem always to be mumbling. You squint. Nothing really works well; I have a friend who takes an inventory of all his movable parts every morning and rates his body accordingly. *B* minus is about the best he ever hopes for.

So—no sudden horseback riding. No avoidable late nights. No drinking after dinner, a ritual that can trigger a surge of artificial energy likely to prolong evenings beyond midnight and to destroy the next day. Looking back a few decades, I wonder why we all stayed up so late: so few really enjoyable things happen after midnight, and so many embarrassing ones. Fortunately, most of the latter get lost in our memory banks; but I can still recall a small dinner party given by Humphrey and Betty Bogart in Beverly Hills back in 1957. Just as we were switching from after-dinner brandy to highballs, Jimmy McHugh, the composer, sat down at the piano, and Judy Garland and Frank Sinatra wandered over and began singing a medley of old ones. When they got to "Bye, Bye Blackbird" I remember exclaiming, "I know the words to that one!" as I draped my arms around their shoulders. Since my voice is even worse than my golf game, I wish to this day I had a picture of our trio and the expressions on their faces.

I've had more embarrassing moments than that; so have we all. But since so many of them occur late at night, we can at least minimize them in middle age by getting to bed earlier. It's also the best precaution against hangovers. The minor infirmities of this time of life are, in certain respects, like hangovers. They must be stoically endured, most of them go away in time, and they should not be discussed or complained about. Midlife miseries arouse no sympathy whatsoever, especially among younger people; in fact, they are more likely to evoke anger and exasperation—as though you were acting infirm on purpose. Ask the deaf: no one feels particularly sorry for the hard-of-hearing—merely annoyed at having to shout and repeat. Or consider your own emotions when dutifully visiting someone in a nursing home for the very old.

These are also the insomnia years: we no longer stay up until 4:00 A.M. but we often wake up then, or even sooner, sometimes in the throes of a dream so complicated that consciousness comes as a welcome respite. "Dreams," we are told by sociobiologist Edward O. Wilson, "are produced when giant fibers in the brainstem fire upward through the brain during sleep, stirring the cerebral cortex to activity. In the absence of ordinary sensory information from the outside, the cortex responds by calling up images from the memory banks and fabricating plausible stories." Barely plausible sometimes, peopled with an improbable cast of characters, fraught with bizarre adventures, and as evanescent as smoke rings. We have all experienced the panic of trying to find the elusive classroom where we are supposed to be taking an exam in a course for which we haven't cracked a book; we have all repeatedly missed planes and trains, lost our baggage or our way in strange cities, and forgotten our lines before hostile audiences. Rumania, for some curious reason, was dream country to me until I went to Bucharest in 1976, actually lost my bags, damn near missed a plane connection, and thereby apparently purged Rumania from the vaults of my subconscious.

In short, sleep—which is usually instant, automatic, and profound in youth—becomes harder to achieve in middle age, harder to sustain and less refreshing because often troubled by laborious dreams. Well, so it goes, as Kurt Vonnegut used to say. Insomnia, we know, is a symptom, not a disease. But a symptom of what? We may uncover some clues as we continue this expedition. Meanwhile, don't sweat it, join the crowd and take a Valium. Or read a book.

These are the years when, as the French say, *"on se tâte,"* a phrase best translated as constantly taking one's pulse. That's why you need a doctor more than ever who is highly skilled, on call in an emergency, up to date professionally, sympathetic to your serious complaints but not inclined to pamper your hypochondria. These superdoctors—that minority of the medical profession who read the journals, trust their intuition, refer you to the very best specialists, and can be depended upon when you really need them—are not all that hard to find. One good way is to ask a physician friend whom *he* would consult if he got sick in your community.

I mentioned hypochondria; it can be crippling, and part of a good doctor's job is to dispel groundless fears. I have an old friend, call him Tom, who worries unduly about his heart. This brings on irregular heartbeats, which in turn aggravate the worry. One day, Tom and I were playing tennis with his doctor, who doesn't like losing. After Tom had raced across the court to drop the game-winning shot just over the net, Doc said with mock concern and a wink at me, "Don't overdo it, chum." Tom was frozen at the baseline during the next set, which we lost, but later got the message better than if the doctor had solemnly told him it was "all in his mind." Psychosomatic disorders, from asthma to vertigo, come and go with such frequency in middle age that you eventually learn to shrug them off. But there are a few major illnesses whose consequences, if you recover, include a permanent if subdued awareness of your own plumbing and wiring as well as a keen ear for any suspicious knocks or squeaks in the machinery.

And middle age is the time of these big killer diseases that put you "in hospital," sometimes in intensive care units; heart attacks, strokes, and cancer head the list. These and a few others—multiple sclerosis, Parkinson's disease, crippling accidents—are the ones that leave the survivors "different." As the old New England saying goes, "They have seen the elephant and heard the hooty owl."

The after-forty diseases that left their visible and invisible marks on me were polio, two heart attacks, a depression, and something called aphasia fugat, which is like a two-minute stroke that comes and goes but leaves an unforgettable calling card behind in your memory. These experiences of mine may cheer you up if you've never had a serious disease but have reason to expect one—and who doesn't?—and they may also make you feel better if you too are an alumnus or alumna of an intensive care unit.

Since the aftereffects of paralytic polio resemble those of a stroke, and since the stroke season starts in middle age just as the hurricane season where I live starts in late summer, let me walk you through a case history that began in the airport of Abidjan, capital of the Ivory Coast, on July 30, 1961. I was just forty-two, not an age to worry about what used to be called infantile paralysis, so I attributed a sudden, buzzing, feverish headache to flu or fatigue after a conference I'd been attending in Nigeria, or both. Besides, in the tropics, you get used to strange, transient fevers. So when we reached Conakry, Guinea, where I was United States ambassador, I took some aspirin and went to bed. But the next afternoon, feeling worse, I checked in with the only European doctor in town, a Frenchman. He diagnosed my trouble as a touch of malaria; I had probably forgotten to take my regular dose of Atabrine. He gave me some pills and told me to go home and rest.

We lived in a bungalow by the palm-fringed ocean. In the morning, walking out to the veranda, my left leg suddenly buckled and I fell down. Diallo, our cook, and Mamadou, the houseboy, picked me up and carried me to bed. By nightfall, my leg was as limp as a string of spaghetti and I had trouble lifting my left arm. The headache was worse. The doctor came, looked perplexed, and said something about a virus. I pushed away the thought of polio; I'd taken Salk shots, hadn't I? Three bad days later, an ambulance took Sim and me to the airport, where I was lifted aboard the regular DC-4 flight to Dakar like a side of beef and dumped into a seat. The paralysis had not spread but the fever persisted.

At Dakar our ambassador, Phil Kaiser, and his wife met us with an ambulance from the French military hospital. There, a quiet and reassuring doctor examined me and did a spinal tap. When he came back later, with Sim, I could see she had been crying. "Is it serious?" I asked. I still could not or would not accept the obvious. He smiled. "You'll be all right," he said. "It will just take some time." I looked at Sim. "Polio?" She nodded. I felt strangely relieved: my enemy was identified, the damage was contained, and from now on it was just a matter of fighting my way back. Hell, the worst was over, and I

could still move my head and all of my right side. I
remember falling asleep almost peacefully, looking forward to the campaign ahead.

The campaign was no blitzkrieg. Immobilized muscles
atrophy like butter melts, and the road back is uphill all
the way. After a week in Dakar, my fever gone, I was carried onto a Pan Am flight to New York. Had I been in
the armed forces, a special military plane would have eva-
cuated me straight back to Washington; but the State
Department always had a lean budget. Since even a month
later I was too weak to sit up, the nine-hour flight was a
nightmare of muscular cramps and fainting spells. But
we made it to Idlewild, then to La Guardia by ambulance,
then on to a flight to Washington, then by ambulance to
Bethesda Naval Hospital—and somehow I checked in alive.
Because an ambassador's equivalent rank in the navy is
rear admiral, I got a private room on the sixteenth "deck."

For the next six weeks I worked: first, muscles that had
gone into spasm had to be straightened out in a water tank
by navy corpsmen. ("Don't scream, sir, until you have
to.") Then, for an hour or two a day, each muscle had to
be moved and gradually coaxed into moving itself. They
sat me in a chair until I got dizzy; strapped me upright on
a tilt table until I got dizzy, wheeled me to the therapy
room until I got dizzy. And cheered me on.

"Hey, Pete! Look at those triceps--they're moving! His
arm's going up! Attaboy, sir!" The corpsmen were extraor-
dinary. Without their enthusiasm, it might have been
tempting on some days—sweaty, trembling with strain,
blue in the face, no progress—just to lie back and quit. But
they never let up, thank God, and kept me struggling
until, late in October, I was finally promoted to out
patient.

There had been plenty of visitors and well-wishers. Some of the regulars, like Joe Alsop, I'll always remember as friends. Others, from far away, wrote letters. Some I was surprised to hear from. And there were others I was surprised not to hear from. A serious illness—one that might put you out of commission and therefore out of useful circulation—does separate the friends from the acquaintances.

The best visitors were those like Ben Bradlee or Tom Sorensen who had had polio and recovered; their encouragement was precious. The worst were those who arrived awash with sympathy, something I didn't need; all I wanted to hear was that I'd be walking again if I worked hard enough.

Almost as unwelcome were visitors who wanted to talk about their problems. Maybe they thought I'd be cheered up to hear that they had troubles too. Troubles? When you can't get out of bed, out of a chair, out of a bathtub, or off a toilet seat without help you tend to be intolerant, of yourself as well as others. Thus, when I'm inclined to feel sorry for myself, I've found it helpful to think back to that sixteenth deck at Bethesda where getting those triceps and quads and inverters and abductors and hip flexors to move again seemed like the only problem I would ever have or that would ever matter. Nor are all the memories painful: I like remembering all the friends who took the trouble to come by; and the tapping of Sim's heels as she came down the corridor every noon; and finding Peter and Jan waiting one day as I rolled out off the elevator in my wheelchair; and knowing at last that I would walk again, maybe not too well, but walk.

The world outside can be scary. On our first outing, to dinner at the Sargent Shrivers', I looked with despair at the three steps that led to their front door. How could

I make it up there on my crutches? Inside, I sought out a high, straight chair, fearing I could never get out of a low one. A few days later, when we moved into John Lindsay's house in Georgetown, I contemplated the stairs with the same initial dread, but with Sim pushing from behind I managed to haul myself up. By November, invited to a White House luncheon, I made it up the front steps, not caring if I fell or not.

Between visits to the hospital I practiced walking with crutches on the crooked red brick sidewalks of Georgetown, and in time managed a block or two with just a cane. But getting out of chairs was still a problem. One day, Sim left me sitting in the garden while she went shopping. It began to rain, which seemed to stimulate pigeon droppings. Of course I could no more get out of my chair than levitate. So by the time Sim returned, I felt and probably looked like a stained and weathered old lawn statue; and considerably more ill-tempered.

By December I was ready to go back to Africa, where I could do my daily therapy out under the palms and swim in the warm Atlantic. Improvement was slow but steady. Peter kept score while Sim added the weights on to my metal boot in quarter-pound increments, and the Guinean soldier assigned to guard our residence looked on in fascination at our bizarre rituals. One day in January I forgot my cane as I escorted a visitor to the door of the embassy; and in March I flew home for a check-up at Bethesda. When I walked—limping but unsupported—into the physiotherapy room where I had agonized through so many sessions, the whole staff crowded around, as delighted as I was. For it had been their victory as much as mine.

A weak left foot and leg, a slight limp. Another year of therapy. In retrospect, no big deal. Now I'm just extra careful crossing streets, I don't try to rush the net at tennis,

I hit the golf ball off my right foot, and I sit out the dances. And when I meet people who are handicapped, I know better than to treat them as if they were, well, different. The only important way in which they might be different is that they are probably tougher: some are overcompensating for a wheelchair, others found unexpected strength in having fought back against heavy odds. And by the way, if you should happen to play tennis with me, don't ever say "sorry" if you manage to hit a ball out of my reach.

Heart attacks are another matter. They leave you not necessarily stronger but usually wiser—that is, more acutely aware of your body's fragility and life's impermanence. If you are like most of us, heart attacks are things that happen to other people. Hypochondriacs aside, most middle-aged people—no matter how overweight or overworked, no matter how high their blood pressure or cholesterol level, no matter how much they smoke or how little they exercise—simply do not expect to be hit by a myocardial infarct, which is what happens when part of your heart muscle dies for lack of blood from one or more occluded coronary arteries.

Yet the odds aren't all that long. More than 1,200,000 Americans will have a heart attack this year, and about 700,000 of them will die. Well, you say, it's a good thing there's no history of it in my family. And then you get zapped—the way I did. Heart attacks aren't all the same, but here's what you may expect.

On September 27, 1967, I called Sim from my room in the Berkshire Hotel in New York just before going to what was certain to be a boring evening at the Overseas Press Club, of which I was vice-president. I felt weary, which was not unusual after a day's toil on Madison

Avenue, and said I wished I were home. She told me to buck up and have a drink, it wouldn't be all that bad.

So I walked the thirteen blocks to the club, reflecting en route that I should never have taken on this extracurricular chore, considering the heavy year I'd just put in, In January there were negotiations in Hamburg over the controversial *Death of a President* book, followed by stopovers in East and West Africa to tape television interviews with Jomo Kenyatta and Sekou Toure; in March and April, a series of jet flights around the country, promoting my just-published book on Africa at literary luncheons, autograph parties, midnight radio interviews, and early morning television talk shows—seventeen appearances in one day alone in Los Angeles; in May, a trip to Moscow to arrange the coverage for a special issue of *Look* on the fiftieth anniversary of the Russian Revolution, then on to India, Thailand, and Vietnam with Sim, watching the war from helicopters and listening politely to United States military propaganda; and on to Japan, Hawaii, and back to New York just in time to talk about my world travels at the first of eighteen *Look* advertising lunches—a road show that again took me to the West Coast and back with late night stops coming and going. And then, at the end of June, I started a fragmented, rainy vacation in a rented seaside cottage filled with hordes of obstreperous and usually surly teenagers—from where I commuted, almost with relief, to my New York office.

I felt chronically tired, my cholesterol was elevated, I suffered occasional discomfort while exercising (didn't everybody?), but I'd stopped cigarettes, wasn't overweight, my blood pressure was normal, and my parents, still healthy at eighty-four and seventy-nine, had no history of heart trouble. So, like most forty-eight-year-olds, I simply took that great pulsating muscle in my chest for granted.

I arrived at the club a little late, time for just one stiff drink before the traditional overdone roast beef, weak coffee, and call to order. I leaned back and was suddenly conscious of a spreading pressure in my chest and back. I'd had similar symptoms a couple of years before in Kenya; they lasted a minute or two, and a British doctor had shrugged them off as unimportant. But this time the minutes went by and the pressure didn't abate. I excused myself, feeling a compulsion to walk, which is a typical heart attack reaction—the victim seeks, somehow, to leave the scene of the pain. In the elevator the pressure became a sharp ache between the shoulder blades, and suddenly I had to urinate.

Back from the men's room and into the lobby, I knew I was in some kind of serious trouble. The ache was now piercing and I was sweating. I told the desk clerk I needed a doctor. He looked at me dubiously; he didn't know a doctor but would call an ambulance. I slumped down in an easy chair outside the bar and loosened my tie. The pain and sweating were worse. People glanced at me, probably thinking I was drunk, and moved on. Talking, for me, was by now a great effort, and besides, there's this desire—when you're sick or in trouble of some kind—not to be conspicuous. (I've heard of swimmers in distress not yelling for the lifeguard, preferring to risk drowning than to make a scene.) Finally, a woman who'd been at the meeting turned up and saw the shape I was in. While she wiped the moisture from my face, someone called the club doctor.

And what was I thinking about all this time? Nothing, really; the pain blotted out thought. Since it was mostly in my back and not in my chest, I had a reason to reject the possibility of a heart attack: this was just something mysterious and very bad, and please, let it be over soon.

The doctor arrived, did a quick examination, and led me to his car just as the police ambulance turned up. They argued over who would take me away and somehow I scrawled a signature on a release for the cops.

At his office, the doctor did an electrocardiogram, took my blood pressure again, and said, "It's got something to do with your heart. Let's go."

On the way down to St. Vincent's Hospital, in Greenwich Village, I began feeling better and found myself talking animatedly, as if this would keep the pain away. On arrival, he got a wheelchair (I protested, of course—wheelchairs connoted prolonged illness, and besides I now felt okay) and wheeled me very rapidly to the intensive care unit, where a bevy of quiet, solicitous nurses got me into bed, put an oxygen mask over my face, and took another electrocardiogram. I felt no great apprehension, even though I knew it was a heart thing, only relief at being in professional hands and a feeling, as I had in Dakar, that the worst was over.

In the night I couldn't sleep, and a pleasant young doctor sat by the bed and talked reassuringly about what had happened—a probable myocardial infarct—and why I should relax now that the period of maximum risk had passed. In fact, it hadn't; I was halfway through a two-stage heart attack, the second part occurring almost painlessly three days later when the occlusion actually did its damage, causing a considerable flurry among the nurses monitoring my heart action on the closed-circuit screen.

The next two weeks in hospital weren't unpleasant, except for being hooked up to the monitoring wires, and being the only survivor in a three-bed ward. Both my neighbors died on different nights, and the sight of the empty beds was unsettling, especially after having heard their doctors giving them hearty, reassuring reports. When mine came in the day my last roommate was carted off, I told him I was getting superstitious. "Tell me anything," I said, "except that I'm doing just fine."

Sim came every day, as she had at Bethesda; and when I was moved out of the intensive care unit and into a private room, visitors turned up. But they were tiring, because I found myself making an effort to entertain them, knowing they regarded me—as I had heart patients in the past—like a fragile piece of broken crockery, only lightly glued together.

Finally the two weeks were up, I was wheeled out into the world, and Sim drove me home where, faint with weakness, I toppled back into bed. It would be some time yet before I could walk comfortably down the driveway to the mailbox, but the thing was behind me. I'd learned what everybody learns after a heart attack: it's not the end of the world as you knew it. Later, I'd learn it need not cramp your life either. But I'd also learn that the worst was by no means over.

Three months of convalescence is ample, and I planned to go back to work after the end of the year. Meanwhile, in December, friends asked me to come down to the Bahamas for some nonstrenuous golf and swimming. It was an enjoyable week: I didn't even think of myself as a cardiac case; not consciously. But when they left me at the airport and I'd gone to the departure lounge, something happened. I panicked.

Percy Knauth, in his book about his own depression, called *A Season in Hell,* came as close as anyone I know to describing the symptoms of what we now know is a common—and curable—biochemical disorder. But even he failed to communicate what it's like when it happens. He hints at it by saying that the one thing that saved him from suicide was the knowledge that *he could commit suicide*— in other words, that there was, as a last resort, an escape from the horror that envelops the victim of depression. The affliction can be triggered by a variety of psychic shocks—the death of someone you love, the sudden breakup of a long marriage, getting fired from an important job, suffering a major illness. One reason people are depression prone in middle age is that this is when things of this sort are most likely to happen.

Anyway, I panicked in Nassau but managed to board the plane and huddled in my seat all the way to New York. By then, the paralyzing fear had lifted, but I checked in with my doctor the next day. In simplified layman's language, what had happened—and would happen again—is that my subconscious mind was by no means convinced that I'd really recovered from my heart attack. So it sounded an alarm to all cells in my body that a Damoclean sword was hanging over us and might drop at any moment.

The next alarm went off just before the New Year. Sim and the children were skiing in Massachusetts, and I was alone in the house. Snow started falling. I lit a fire, poured a drink, and turned on the television. Then I thought: what if I got snowed in? Could an ambulance get up the long driveway? Could . . . zap. I got to the phone, called Sim, and asked her to come home right away and tried to explain why. She told me to relax (relax!), that they were already snowed in and would be back in a couple of days. I made it through the night—you always do—and went back to the doctor in the morning. He gave me Valium and told me my symptoms were not unusual.

But did I want to see a psychiatrist? No; there was nothing one could tell me that I didn't already know, rationally.

But then, during the winter and spring, I suffered more bad spells—one on a beach in Haiti where I'd gone for a weekend with Jan and a friend (I swam out, almost too far, to conceal the panic) ; another on the New Canaan golf course (could I make it back to the clubhouse?) ; another in a New York hotel room, changing my shirt to go to a dinner party (I excused myself and made my way home instead) ; and another in Cambodia, where Sim and I had gone to interview Prince Sihanouk after seeing Nasser in Egypt. Working travel, I figured, would help my recovery. On the way home, I stopped in New Delhi—Sim had gone on home—to meet Indira Gandhi. In the night I woke up with chest pains; they turned out to be psychosomatic.

Enough. In May, I checked into a New York hospital for ten days to be treated with an antidepressant drug. Within a month I could recall the symptoms as dimly as one remembers an old nightmare. It was as if I'd been trapped in a noxious fog that all at once burnt off. Naturally no one congratulated me on my recovery; depression is a kind of secret illness for which you can expect no sympathy, perhaps because there are no visible wounds or obvious suffering.

I mentioned psychiatrists. I suppose that for some people who have nobody they can talk to intimately, a psychiatrist can be helpful when depression hits if only as a source of reassurance and to suggest tricks for coping with it until it's established that your problem is more biochemical than emotional. But my limited experience with psychiatrists has left me with the impression that very few are worth the fees they charge. The best dispense common sense to the distraught and desperate; the worst sign them up for years of therapy or analysis. I had a friend who after eight years of analysis started yelling at the waiter one day at lunch. "It's my shrink's idea," he explained apologetically. "He told me I need to be more assertive."

If I thought I needed a psychiatrist, I'd go to Switzerland, where the object seems to be to cure you and get rid of you as quickly as possible. At thirty-four, back from an exhausting five-month assignment around the world, I went to a sanatorium in Switzerland—the one where Zelda Fitzgerald was treated in the twenties—suffering from nervous tension and insomnia. After four weeks of physical and psychiatric testing, therapy and enforced rest, I was discharged, comfortably unwound. I remember the chief psychiatrist saying, "You're perfectly healthy—no emotional problems except for a predictable mild anxiety neurosis." Predictable? "It's characteristic of your profession," he explained. "All journalists have mild anxiety neuroses."

For the rest of 1968 I didn't think too much about my damaged heart. I had no pain or discomfort. I dieted, probably not enough; exercised, probably not enough; worried about my teenage children, probably too much; and commuted five days a week to New York.

Then, early in January, 1969, I got hit again.

It happened while playing paddle tennis—pains, this time in my chest, but not as acute as in 1967. A friend drove me home, where I sat by the phone, sweating (a bad sign), but still trying to believe that this was something else that would go away. It didn't. I called Sim, who called our doctor, who came and confirmed that something—the electrocardiogram and transaminase test were "equivocal"—was happening to my heart.

And so, less than eighteen months after my New York

"coronary event" I was back in an intensive care unit, wired to the monitor, oxygen mask in place, for another two weeks of recuperation. The attack turned out to be what they call mild, but it was a second one nonetheless. This meant permanent daily medication and a solemn lecture about diet, fatigue, and overexertion, ending with a prognosis that with a little luck I could probably look forward to five more years on spaceship earth.

Ten days out of hospital, I returned for a catheterization, a forty-five-minute procedure whereby a flexible tube is inserted in an artery in your arm and threaded up and into your heart. Dye is then squirted in and X-rays taken that reveal to what extent the coronary arteries that nourish the heart are blocked or narrowed. The cardiologist who did the job decided that mine were in such sorry shape that bypass surgery was essential, and he booked me into the Cleveland Clinic for what they called a lateral implant.

I was by now resigned to almost anything, but Sim wisely urged me to take my X-rays to St. Vincent's Hospital, where the doctors were already acquainted with my heart, and get a second opinion. It was a good thing she insisted. After a series of tests, electrocardiograms, and walking up a treadmill, I was advised to cancel the surgery, take my medication, get plenty of exercise, and call them if I ever got persistent chest pains.

That was thirteen years ago, and I haven't had to call them yet.

I still remember how sparkling and vibrant the streets of New York looked as I walked out of the hospital. Death's messenger, Mr. Thanatos, who I felt for some weeks had been lurking around, was nowhere in sight.

Nor did I experience the depression that had gripped me a year earlier, perhaps because I'd grown accustomed to living with that Damoclean sword, and the addition of another over my head didn't make so much difference. So I spent my convalescence writing a children's book that was published in the fall, and went back to work in March.

What happened, and how has my life been affected since? The real question here is: how will yours be?

What happened is that I developed collateral arteries—which are like tunnels that the body drills to get around a blocked coronary and keep blood flowing to the heart. Exercise helps keep these collaterals open and functioning by making the heart beat faster and call for more blood. When it doesn't get it, angina pains result—which I occasionally have at the start of a tennis game. Doctors call this walk-through angina because it fades away as the collaterals go to work.

And how have my coronary events changed the way I live? Aside from reinforcing my exercise habit, they've taught me to pull the plugs, so to speak, on highly charged emotional situations. For example, in 1969, a bad year for parents of teenagers, I learned how to become a spectator rather than a participant in dangerous domestic turbulence, such as mother-daughter quarrels. An instinct of self-preservation would tell me a fight was going on—over there. I'd feel sorry, but my blood pressure would hold steady at 120/80. When Jan and Peter joined the throng who consecutively and temporarily embraced noisy activism, passive dropping out, faddist rebellion, pot, communes, and the like, that old life-preserving impulse enabled me to adopt not a so-what but rather a so-it-goes attitude. I didn't become a less caring parent, simply a less agitated one; and consequently, perhaps a better one. But that's for them to judge.

And so, fourteen years have gone by since that traumatic evening at the Overseas Press Club, and I'm okay. I guess I'm okay. I do just about everything I want. But not a day has gone by that I haven't been aware that there is a heart pumping away in my chest, and that a part of it is dead.

One more scare and we're through.

Just before midnight on February 5, 1980, I woke from a troubled half-sleep and turned over on my side. Or tried to. I couldn't seem to make it. I grunted. Sim woke up. I made a moaning noise. "You're having a bad dream," she said. I made another noise. She turned on the light. "What's the matter?" I found I couldn't talk, only make sounds. "Give me your hand," she said. I couldn't move it. I realized I couldn't move my right leg either. She got out of bed and hurried to the kitchen phone. Her mother had had a stroke, and she knew the symptoms.

I lay there, knowing only that something had happened—again. But I felt no panic, not even anxiety. I lifted my limp right arm with my left hand—an old polio reflex—and placed it on my chest. It began to tingle. When Sim came back, the fingers were moving. We looked at each other. "I can talk again, too," I said.

Our doctor arrived in a few minutes. His first word was cryptic: "garbagio." After giving me some injections, he explained what he meant: loose plaque from a hardened artery had probably shut off, momentarily, one of the carotid arteries leading to the brain and given me a fleeting stroke. It even had a name: aphasia fugat. So now I'd had a glimpse of *that* specter, and it was the worst.

The next few weeks were haunted by apprehension. Despite anticoagulant drugs, I had spells of blurred vision and dizziness—indications of neurological trouble. I was given a brain scan: normal. I saw a neurosurgeon: he suspected an ulcerating plaque, in which case a not-so-routine operation would be necessary. Sim drove me to Columbia Presbyterian Hospital in New York for an angiogram—which is like a catheterization except that the tube is inserted in the groin and the dye squirts into your neck and head. It lasts more than an hour, it's scary, and it hurts. But it tells the surgeon what he needs to know.

When I was wheeled back upstairs, Sim, Peter, Jan and Suzy were waiting in my room. We'd get the verdict the next day. I was tired, so they didn't stay long. But seeing them gathered around, the concern showing in their expressions and embraces, I reflected that a life-endangering illness does bring the love out in a family, particularly among us normally undemonstrative Anglo-Saxons. Perhaps we should express our deep-down emotions more often to each other; perhaps not. Love restrained but revealed on special occasions can be felt more intensely than love on permanent display. Anyway, I was crying when they left, and I don't cry often, not even at the movies.

Aphasia fugat had a happy ending. The angiogram showed that an operation would not be necessary. The blurred vision faded away and the dizzy spells eventually yielded to a prescription drug. I am working now at the desk where I first felt some dizziness the day before the semistroke—and that was many months ago.

So let me wind up this recital of sickness with a few observations appropriate to middle age.

First, there are a lot of minor but persistent ailments peculiar to this time of life that simply must be endured; unexplained aches, pains, and twinges are just part of the aging process. You can always rejoice on those good days when the symptoms subside a bit, and after those good nights when you wake feeling reasonably refreshed.

Second, the life-endangering illnesses have positive as

well as negative consequences—assuming of course that you survive them with only moderate damage to your system.

On the negative side is the heightened awareness of one's own wiring and plumbing and their irreversible deterioration, and also of one's ever-approaching, perhaps even imminent, death. It's something you learn to live with, but it does set you apart from those who haven't heard the hooty owl.

On the positive side, you develop a keener appreciation of how precious is life itself and the enjoyment of it; of how silly quarrels—especially marital quarrels—can be (for who else but she—or he—really cares?) ; of how unimportant are the troubles most people complain about (as I learned in my wheelchair in Bethesda) ; of how to be detached and to retreat to that calm center that exists deep in us all whenever emotional storm clouds make their appearance.

One final generalization: killer diseases don't improve anyone's sex life. Thinking about your pulse rate inhibits the total submersion so necessary to sex, but it also inhibits adultery (one does worry about dying in the wrong bed) ; and that, as we may determine in the next chapter, may not be a bad thing at all.

4

SEX

EVERYBODY WHO HAS TRIED to play golf for a long time, as I have, knows that when you address the ball with the slightest doubt in your mind about hitting it straight and true, it is almost certain to be a bad shot: either you top it, plough under it, or send it in the wrong direction. You also learn, as time goes by, that, while imagination and concentration are all-important just before impact, it's best not to think too much about the score. In fact, you may reach the point, if you're lucky enough, to acquire such a high handicap that you can stop thinking about the score altogether and proceed to play the game purely for the exercise, the scenery, and the companionship. If you manage to hit four or five good shots in a row and par or birdie a hole or two, that's only frosting on the cake.

Sex is like golf, especially in the years we are concerned with here: a lot of it is in the head, and the pleasure of stroking a really clean drive, like achieving a well-timed orgasm, is certainly intense though distressingly short-lived. "Do you want to exchange ten minutes of rapture for a lifetime of regret?" was the classic crescendo of the old-time United States Army venereal disease lecture. "Sir," was the legendary first question, "how do you make it last ten minutes?"

Golf is a good deal trickier and more complex and much harder to master than sex, but the analogy—if I don't press it too far—is at least sufficiently apt to have got me launched on this minefield of a chapter.

Just about everyone is interested in sex, some idly, some sporadically, some immoderately. A few, who are able to feel fully alive only during intercourse, can be understandably obsessive about it: I don't think this chapter is for them. The people I see in the audience during this episode are for the most part middle-aged men and women who still think that sex is more fun than anything else two people can do without laughing.

Most of us, I've noticed, pass through three stages in our approach to sex. In youth, it's both a problem to be coped with and an activity to be indulged in whenever opportunities arise, which they do now with greater frequency than in my own fervent but frustrated adolescence; later on, sex can be a source of restlessness as the familiar conjugal rituals cease to excite; and still later, a kind of resignation often sets in, and sex—after perhaps one final and usually disappointing escapade—is appreciated as part of a larger canvas, so to speak, and enjoyed, like those relaxed rounds of erratic golf, for the exercise, the scenery, and the companionship.

If we stay with the forty-plus definition of middle age, this is the period of your life when you think more about sex than at any time since the teens. Recalling the lyrics of Kurt Weill's "September Song," you wonder about October and November and whether pretty soon it's going to be all over; or is there time left to play out one final fantasy? The specter of impotence lurks head—ever since that night when, at thirty-nine, after six highballs, you weren't able to perform as expected. You remember silly jokes about old sugar daddies making fools of themselves. You suspect—hell, you *know*—that you will soon be regarded without the slightest flicker of interest by young and attractive women. On sleepless nights you recall and deeply regret all those missed opportunities not seized during your gloriously untrammeled youth; but never, repeat never, do you regret the ones seized and embraced no matter how embarrassing and even ludicrous they turned out to be.

In Des Moines, years ago, a rich old man lay dying. His relatives kept silent vigil, making appropriate conversation whenever he exhibited signs of lucidity. "You've had a wonderful life, grandpa," said one of them at such a moment. "Would you live it any differently if you had another chance?" And the old man's son told me the reply was: "Yep. I wouldn't have worried so much about gettin' the clap." All of the ones he'd missed—of course that's what was going through his mind in those last few hours of sentient life.

I remember them, too, on some nights, starting back when I was barely fifteen and sharing a rowboat in the harbor of Port Jefferson, New York, with a precocious fourteen-year-old blonde whom I'd invited to go fishing. Suddenly, while baiting the lines, I noticed her removing the top of her bathing suit. Did I mind, she asked, if she took a real good sunbath? I was too stunned to reply; I simply rammed a fishhook through my thumb. Finally, sensing something was expected of me, I edged forward to the bow, leaned over, and kissed her. (Why didn't she respond? My whole life might have been different.) Then, overcome with embarrassment, I dived overboard and swam furiously to shore, leaving her to weigh anchor and row the boat back alone.

I was not alone in my naiveté. A lot of us in the thirties suffered from the delusion that girls resented being touched and in fact only humored us with indifferent kisses as a kind of distasteful (to them) reward for our asking them out for a chocolate malted and a double feature at the Bijou theater. We missed a lot, many of us, and still brood, years later, over certain recollected idiocies.

But youthful memories that do involve sexual fulfillment, however squalid, usually elicit neither remorse nor regret, at least in the male animal. In Luxembourg, in 1946, I left two pleasant and not unattractive American Red Cross girls in a hotel after dinner to go prowling around the bars until I finally found a slovenly, compliant *fräulein* left behind by Hitler's retreating panzers a year earlier. I slinked back in the dawn like a weary tomcat to confront the silent scorn of my American companions all the way back to Frankfurt. Hangover, sure; regrets, none. None either for the time I woke up in a fourth-class hotel in Montmartre with not one but two bedraggled young birds of prey; we were joined by the lady receptionist who brought up a bottle of champagne and prolonged our slumber party into the daylight hours. I look back on such experiences as things worth doing just a few times and early in life, if only to get them out of the way and not have to wonder later if you might have missed something important by marrying your prom date right after graduation.

Living in Paris as a bachelor in the forties made it easy to indulge in casual and exploratory sex that may well have saved me from a good deal of fantasizing and even foolishness later on. We finished our work at the New York *Herald Tribune* around 10:00 P.M., too late for any conventional social life, and spent many of our evenings with the young war widows, small-time gangsters, and semipro entertainers who frequented the nearby bars. The subways stopped running at 1:00 A.M. so that those girls unable to make a good connection by that time would occasionally stay over at my apartment up the street from the paper. Amicable sex was of course part of the arrangement, along with the making of breakfast and maybe a little vacuuming and laundering. It was not a bad deal, all around, though my social circle in those days was fairly restricted and did not overlap with the world of Parisian high society. But I doubt if I missed much.

And of course it paid off in camaraderie; once, when I did some girls a favor by escorting them into the Lido night club—women alone had been banned in a futile attempt to discourage pickups—a waiter rushed up with a bottle of high-priced champagne. "But he's not an American!" cried one of my flock. "He's a pal—he's one of us!" We drank Perrier instead. It was nice to feel accepted.

The point of citing these Parisian follies is that I was able to learn enough about whores in those days not to be tempted in middle age—as a good many men are—by call girls, massage parlors, sex spas, and the like. When I read about fictional happy hookers, and Hugh Hefner's house parties, I think of a frail, sad-eyed young Spanish prostitute in a bar-bordello in Tangiers. "All time for me is fack, fack, fack," she told me wearily. "But me no like fack." That's more like reality.

The middle years are also, paradoxically, a period of burgeoning sexual opportunity for many men. This is when the once elusive and temperamental women we pursued in our youth now beckon like Lorelei—at forty or forty-five—along with certain younger ones who, perhaps for psychological reasons, prefer their men friends older. (Because kinder, wealthier, more fatherly, more experienced, more considerate? On the whole, it's best not to find out.) If you are tempted, married or not, to make the most of these midlife opportunities, then at the very least take care to observe three practical taboos: never with wives of friends, never with fellow employees, and never with women under twenty-five. These three categories are the ones most likely to create all kinds of trouble for the philandering male—indiscretion and emotional complications being the most common.

And yet, for some of us this is also a time when we wonder if our sex life is all it should be. (Wives are probably asking themselves the same question.) The skin books and the raunchy paperbacks refer casually to esoteric delights never experienced and by some of us never even imagined. It is now, too, that the latent perversions and kinkiness that hover deep within us all tend to surface, even if only in dreams: suggestions of homosexuality, pedophilia, incest, sado-masochism. Sometimes they are too strong for suppression or sublimation, in which case there are places where for a little as $100 you can treat yourself to a kind of secret therapy; but generally these inclinations can be dispelled more efficaciously, and economically, through private fantasy.

The French, until the big wide-open brothels were closed by law in 1946, could be epicurean in catering to "special tastes." I knew of houses where the girls were all pregnant, or over seventy, or moronic, or very young and small and sitting in a mock classroom where the customer could play the uninhibited teacher. I saw rooms outfitted like igloos and beach cabanas, or like Pullman compartments for those eccentrics who need the sound and motion of a train as a sexual backdrop.

And the lengths to which some people will go to achieve an orgasm seem to increase with the passing years.

Arranging experimental liaisons with partners who attract you is another pastime not confined to middle age but which certainly is given more consideration at this time of life. From my own observations in the supposedly swinging suburbs, I'd say that cheating, as it used to be called, is far less prevalent in real life than in fiction. One reason is logistics—always an effective deterrent with ubiquitous neighbors and children; another is that not a lot of people have the requisite sex appeal to justify the effort and the risk; and a third reason might derive from Mark Twain's remark that the best defense against temptation is cowardice.

This is not to say that clandestine or illicit sex is exceptional. In fact, I wouldn't bet ten bucks that *any* of my male friends has been consistently faithful, sexually, to his wife, and in a recent *Cosmopolitan* survey, two-thirds of the latter admitted to playing around. But there are varieties of infidelity: the brief encounter on a business trip can't be equated with the mistress in the convenient midtown apartment. The latter requires a degree of emotional schizophrenia that not everyone (not I, certainly) can conjure up unless the marriage itself has become so sterile that the other arrangement becomes the centerpiece.

The brief encounters become more frequent in the middle years because the victim of advancing age requires repeated reassurance, like a fading matinee idol, that the incipient jowls and graying temples have only enhanced his charm. But casual seduction has its own price tag—paid not after cocktails and dinner but usually at three in the morning. That seems to be wake-up time for most philanderers; that's when they lie in the dark, head gently throbbing, in an unfamiliar bed redolent with the unfamiliar scent of a softly-snoring stranger, wondering if anyone (for example, a wife) has been calling the hotel, wishing they were back there, wondering how to get a cab at this hour, searching for black socks on a dark rug, hoping the encountered partner is a sound sleeper or—if wakened—uncommunicative.

Just as nourishing to the ego as the brief encounter—which is provoked more often than not by macho pride as much as by lust—is the knowledge that you *could* seduce a certain desirable woman if you just made a move (there are signals) —and then not make a move. I know several such women, and they know why I don't call them. But I think most of us need to experience the disenchantment of casual sexual encounters as part of the final maturing process that gives middle age its justifications and also its greatest satisfaction—the full appreciation of what married love is all about.

Would I apply all of the foregoing to women? A generation ago, my answer would have been no; today it's a qualified yes—qualified because for all of the changes that have occurred in male-female relations, there are still profound differences in the way men and women think about sex. For example, most women are less casual about it than men, and attach more importance to physical relationships. I've heard it said that, given good sex, women can forgive men anything; deprived of it, they can forgive men nothing. It sounds too glib, like all aphorisms, but it's not too wide of the mark. For most men, sex is certainly the spice of life but seldom the main course. They leaf through *Playboy* but unless they are very young they don't take the Hefner philosophy (fuck as much as you can) very seriously. Most women don't even buy *Playgirl,* though some seem to read a lot of rather pathetic articles about attracting and holding men. "How to Persuade Your Date to Stay for Breakfast" is one that sticks in my mind. The conventional wisdom, that women are more likely than men to romanticize a sexual experience, may be true. I remember arguing with a woman friend for years about Brussels—to me a nondescript city she considered the loveliest in Europe—until I finally learned she'd lost her virginity there in the pleasantest of circumstances.

Romance. Love. I mentioned love a while back, but I think only once so far this chapter that deals with what is sometimes called the act of love. Perhaps we have become too accustomed in this generation to separating sex—increasingly a subject for clinical analysis—from love, a word both quaint and overused. And yet love is or should be an integral part of sex; indeed it is often simulated in order to speed up seduction or invoked for maximum effect at the top of the orgasmic roller coaster. But love as a momentary aphrodisiac is as different from the love that makes the world go round as are a couple of adolescents fumbling with zippers in a parked car from a man and a women expressing in one warm embrace some of their intimacy, their loneliness, their many yearnings, their shared affection, and their trust, in an intensely private act. "Tenderness," said the French poet Joseph Joubert, "is passion in repose." This is the dream, an attainable dream though not attained as often as it should be. Quarrels and boredom intervene. So do children and fatigue and indigestion. But it is still the best of the only two kinds of sexual relationships that make any sense—the other being a quick, impersonal coupling with a total stranger. Anything in between—like affairs (which sound to me as if they should be catered) —is usually disappointing; conversation becomes strained; the unspoken question—where is this leading?—hangs in the air; and the constant deception if one or both of you is married, turns the thing into more of an inconvenience than an adventure. In short, the participants are too close for the lustfully impersonal roll in the hay or on the rug but not likely ever to be close enough for what a French woman once described to me as *"les arabesques du bonheur."*

One exception to this rule might be the openly extra-marital romance, something not uncommon in middle age among people who are badly but irrevocably married. This takes some discretion all around to avoid unnecessary embarrassment as well as some tolerance on the part of the cuckolded spouse or spouses—who almost always know what's happening. But then why not divorce? Only because there may be other factors to consider—children, illness, finances—who knows? There just are . . . factors.

A final comment about adultery—another word, like affair, that I've never liked because it sounds like adding water to the vodka bottle. The brief and casual encounters —which diminish in middle age because they've been tried and found wanting—are no threat to relatively stable marriages; they may even strengthen such marriages as the "guilty" or remorseful party seeks, often clumsily, to make up for his or her transgressions.

The relationships that spouses should be concerned about are the initially platonic one with old friends or business associates of the opposite sex. These can and often do turn into uncatered affairs if the spouse at home fails to provide the companionship which is almost always the missing ingredient that triggered the "friendship" in the first place.

As middle age closes in, you can be thankful if you married late and had ample opportunity to get rid of most of your curiosity about the other gender and the interesting things that people with imagination do in beds. If not, you may decide in your forties and fifties that you absolutely have to find out what you may have missed, erotically, before you're over the hill forever. So you do, and it's almost sure to be a letdown and may even get you into some kind of trouble, depending on how kinky the impulse. Kinky, as defined by Christine Keeler, the star of Britain's biggest sex scandal of the sixties, is "doing anything with anybody anywhere at anytime."

By middle age, certainly, and sometimes much earlier, during a honeymoon, for example, you also discover that marriage isn't a particularly sexy institution. Not because it becomes so routine or so domestic, but rather because your spouse over the years inevitably acquires more and more of the combined attributes of a business partner, an old friend, a nurse, a sister, and a mother. Did you ever notice how many long-married men refer to their wives as "mother"? If you're a woman reading this, just change the sexes; it works both ways. In short, the sexual aspect of marriage can become slightly awkward.

Yet sex remains an essential—if, in due course, attenuated—element of marriage. Attenuated but symbolic, which can be all-important. And it also remains the most affecting form of nonverbal communication between human beings. That's why a marriage that endures with very little or even no sex at all is a marriage gone sour, however sturdy it may appear on the surface. Impotence is often blamed but it is seldom the cause. Fear is. Fear of rejection (which would expose the bankruptcy of the marriage), or fear of a renewed intimacy with all the emotional vulnerability that goes with it. When I was going through a squallish period in my own marriage, I remember talking about it with Betty Bacall, who had endured much rougher times in the years after Bogey's death. "Do you still make love?" was her first question. "Yes? Then it'll probably be okay."

A quotation from a very wise lady like Bacall is as good a way as any to wind up this gingerly crafted disquisition about sex in the autumn years before examing the ups and downs of wedlock.

5

MARRIAGE

OUR GENERATION was the last one weaned on fairy tales and stories that ended with the boy marrying the girl and the two of them living happily ever after. Maybe that's why it took us longer than our sons and daughters to learn that this is not the way it is at all in real life.

I'm not suggesting that it's as bad as I once heard it expressed by Oscar Levant, the celebrated and misanthropic pianist. We were at a party in Beverly Hills when he interrupted a discussion about the wars of the sexes by proclaiming, in a kind of stammering whisper, "Marriage is a—triumph of habit—over hatred."

Too harsh, I would say. A triumph of inertia over boredom comes closer. But why not call it just—a triumph?

For isn't there something triumphant about two people —so different in so many obvious and also subtle ways— staying together through decades of sickness, quarrels, hard times, obstreperous children, incompatibility, menopause, clashing egos, tiresome anecdotes, excessive proximity and deteriorating sex appeal? You bet there is; and about half-way through middle age you begin to appreciate it. That's when it dawns on you that the bonds of love that have kept you together for a quarter century or more are stronger than they seemed, perhaps because love is often unexpressed; and when you know instinctively that neither partner in this strenuous but precious enterprise is going to walk away—not any more. It has survived all the major crises, and you know you are going to stay with it from now on and forget about all those dreams of fresh starts with other mates. You decide at last to make the best of it. And most of us do.

Yet not as many couples as before now last the distance. One half of today's marriages end in divorce. The divorce rate here has almost tripled since the 1930s. Consider my own family: My son Peter has been divorced once, and my niece Yvonne and daughter Jan twice; among the older folks, two of Sim's four siblings have been divorced, along with two of my mother's four living sisters.

I suppose my other relatives, like almost every married couple I've known, have considered divorce or separation at one time or another—even my parents, who still held hands at the movies when they were both past seventy-five. Sim and I are no exception; we've discussed it. One reason palmists and fortune tellers still make a good living is that their "reading" of every new client always includes five statements certain to appeal to nine out of ten people: you have considered a divorce; you have even thought of suicide; your husband (or wife) doesn't appreciate you; you have strange dreams; you are much more sensitive and intelligent than people think.

The reason almost everybody has contemplated divorce is that marriage hardly ever lives up to our expectations, except when we marry for money and have checked out the quarry's financial situation in advance. Money marriages occasionally turn out very well, perhaps because the emotional expectations are limited and the strains accordingly reduced. Consider Mrs. Benjamin Disraeli, the wife of Queen Victoria's favorite prime minister. "I know my husband married me for my money," she said, "but if he were to do it again, it would be for love."

Many marriages weather the rough seas of the late twenties and early thirties because of the catalytic effect of young children. (How can the Easter Bunny walk out on the Tooth Fairy?) Later, of course, adolescent children can create marital havoc (but that's part of another chapter). And by early middle age, unless an overflowing backlog of hatred has accumulated, or an alternative romantic lead has made his or her appearance, the chances are that the combined effect of shared memories, joint possessions, fear of aloneness, and sheer fatigue will steer you both into a tolerably quiet and pleasant harbor for the sunset years.

Memories are important. Most marriages need a stockpile of good ones as shock absorbers during stressful moments. Recollecting the pleasant moments enjoyed together or with the children—climbing a mountain, planting a garden, discovering a new country, laughing over cutthroat croquet—is what keeps many families from drifting irrevocably apart in the darkening mists of middle age. For now is when boredom looms, now when there is more time to talk and, for some couples, fewer things to say. And while boredom doesn't by itself destroy many marriages, it certainly can anesthetize them, which usually comes to the same thing.

Some boredom is inevitable after the children are scattered. Without them to worry about and talk about, some husbands and wives lapse into silence, which is okay if their intimacy is strong enough not to require conversation; others fabricate talk about current events, which can only be stilted, or other people's activities or misfortunes, which tends to be gossipy. That's why a nugget of hard new information—a local bank robbery or suicide, for example—is precious metal for someone facing a meal alone with a spouse of long standing. This is particularly true after retirement, when "what happened at the office today?" can no longer be used by either partner to enliven the occasion.

Boredom in middle age can lead to quarrels, which do at least break the monotony. The anger behind most quarrels, of course, comes from the feeling that the marriage in which you are trapped has lost its savor and excitement. In middle age, the motive for an outburst is more often than not mere frustration. Not all fights, in short, are all bad; in fact, they are preferable in the long run to a disciplined serenity. Fighting denotes emotion, caring, even love. And criticism, which triggers many a quarrel, can often be an expression of caring. As J. B. Priestley once observed, "A loving wife will do anything for her husband except to stop criticizing him and trying to improve him." Few husbands would disagree. But I once heard Chief Justice Earl Warren, in a eulogy, add a perceptive caveat to Priestley's proposition: "Love without criticism," he said, "can be corrosive; but criticism without love is always destructive." What makes so much criticism destructive is that it is normally delivered without noticeable warmth or affection. The man with the loving wife is likely to forget that she's only calling him a lazy incompetent slob because she wants to improve him. And thus are battles joined.

Having had direct and indirect experience with marital combat—both the brief skirmishes and the protracted trench warfare—I am seldom surprised to hear that friends are divorcing or separating. And unless they are young people with children, my impulse is to congratulate them. Young people with children should make a special effort to stick it out for a few years; kids need resident fathers as well as mothers. But the childless young are only cutting their losses and will be none the worse and probably somewhat wiser for having married in haste; and the older couples are doing it in all likelihood because their marriages have become literally intolerable. Otherwise, the ballast of inertia, memories, companionship—all the centrifugal factors I've mentioned—would have kept the marriage from foundering on the uncharted shoals and reefs of middle age. So a divorce is no cause for lamentation. On the contrary, it's usually the most courageous and sensible way out of a very bad situation. Just be sure you don't take sides with either party in a separation, try as both will to recruit you. Middle age is no time to jeopardize old friendships: there aren't that many left to spare.

"Families break up," said Robert Frost, "when people take hints you don't intend and miss hints you do intend." Two everyday examples will suffice to illustrate how easily this can happen. "Is your mother leaving tomorrow?" (no hint intended) is received by the spouse as "I don't want her around." And "Let's have a quiet evening together for change" (hint of possible intimacy intended) is received as "I'm tired of seeing your friends all the time."

The wonder is not that so many couples separate but that so many stick together. People usually express surprise at the news of an unexpected split up, but I suspect that most marriages are in a state of passive or active disintegration at the onset of middle age. Whether the process can be reversed is the challenge we all have had to face, and whether it is worth the effort is the question we have all had to answer.

That's why I said divorces don't surprise me anymore, not even when my son-in-law told my daughter he was leaving her for another woman just three days after having lovingly celebrated their third wedding anniversary at our house. Most people play out the happy couple role to the end; it matters to them to be thought of, and envied, as being happily married. For a broken or dissolving marriage implies fault, blame, guilt, failure. Better to make an effort to conceal the evidence of disharmony. Everyone has noticed that nothing stops a marital quarrel faster than the sudden arrival of a visitor; I have friends who deliberately invite people over to their homes the moment they can see the storm clouds forming. But no amout of play-acting can long disguise a collapsing marriage. There are tell-tale signs: no kisses, very little touching, cold glances, sudden flare ups over minor offenses like a trumped ace, a broken cup, an unmailed letter. In private the contestants are much less civil and circumspect. Walking toward our tennis court one day, I overheard the cheerful couple we'd been playing with as they swept the lines. She: "Don't hold the broom like that. Can't you learn to do anything right?" He: "Why don't you shut up just for a change?"

Occasional disputes, quarrels and even eruptions of hostility are normal in marriage and no cause to call up a counsellor. Sim and I, after thirty-one years of matrimony, have literally fought our way around the globe: I can still recall three days of frosty silence in Marrakech, a bad night and morning in Havana (she finally called from the airport to say goodby), a stretch in the doghouse in Moscow and another in Beirut, and an uncommunicative flight across the Pacific from Hong Kong to Honolulu. I have stalked out of our house in Connecticut from time to time, and once or twice made it all the way to a motel; usually I got no farther than the guest room.

But there are no winners, only losers, in a conjugal fight, since no victory is possible or conceivable over someone you love. So why do they occur and what are they about?

They occur because of pent-up frustrations—because no marriage lives up to its advance billing, let alone our idealized expectations of it; and the fights are about things that have little or nothing to do with whatever triggered the quarrel. In Marrakech, Sim was ostensibly annoyed because I'd left her sitting alone in the hotel bar to talk to the bartender about the best way to drive over the Atlas Mountains; in Havana, she resented my talking to Fidel Castro for two hours in his private plane without inviting her to leave her seat and join us. But in each case—and in other fights whose proximate causes I've forgotten—she was angry at me for neglecting her. She was saying: you don't care about me, you only think of yourself. Married couples are continually crying to each other for attention, for reassurance; and marriages endure when these cries are answered, and break up when they're not.

In middle age, husband-and-wife fights are usually less damaging but potentially more dangerous than in the

earlier years. They are less damaging because both participants know, or should know the rules of combat and the
limits which must be observed. Many fights in fact come
to resemble stylized medieval jousts in which familiar
threats, insults and accusations are exchanged but no one
is seriously wounded or even unhorsed. Women are particularly adept at pulling back when a conventional fight
threatens to become nuclear; they retire from the scene
when their spouses get carried away and risk saying the
things which in all human relationships should be left
unsaid. (I remember Sim once moving to another table at
a New Year's party so as not to hear me express some possibly hurtful half-truths fueled by champagne cocktails.)
Some men also learn to pull the plugs and muffle the
sound when women began sniping at the most vulnerable
areas of the ego—the peculiar Achilles' heels that only
those closest to us know about.

But marital fights in middle age also become more dangerous for at least three reasons: first, because women who
feel less attractive often act less attractive—and reconcilia-
tion through sex becomes less and less likely; second, because drinking is more prevalent, probably because for
some people it momentarily turns back the ticking clock,
and things are said which not only curdle the present but
can poison that reservoir of good memories that holds
marriages together; and third, because the late afternoon
of life is when we more than ever need the life-preserving
warmth of secure and certain love.

Knowing the dangers and the heartbreak of marital
discord in middle age, why do so many of us engage in
endless skirmishing with rusty weapons to no advantage?

"Why don't *you* get up and look for it? I'm always
looking for your things."

"What's that? Why are you mumbling? You mumble all the time."

"I'm *not* mumbling—you're just getting deaf."

"Stop shouting at me—you shout all the time!"

"It's all my fault, as usual."

"I've asked you to put this away a dozen times, why don't you do it? You never do anything I ask."

"Can't you see I'm on the phone? Try not to let the dog bark so much when I'm talking to somebody."

"Now what is it? Can't you see I'm in a hurry?"

"You shouldn't have had so much to drink."

"Shall we talk about it in the morning?"

"I'm tired. . . . I have a headache. . . . Why don't you just go to sleep. . . . Why don't you . . . Why . . ."

What sustains this futile struggle to gain the upper hand which, if ever achieved, would doom a marriage? The browbeaten wife and the henpecked husband exist as mute and tragic testimony of what happens when one partner finally withdraws from the battle and accepts the hegemony of his or her mate (who, in truth, never really wanted it).

Most partners don't surrender, although they may disengage, at least emotionally. So why is the struggle sustained and even intensified in middle age? Why did one of our women friends punish her husband's infidelity by making herself more physically unattractive? Why did another react by becoming unhappily promiscuous at forty-five? Because insecurity, loneliness and frustration drive people to irrational behavior that is often contrary to their own best interests. Because they married wrong and early and blame their mates for the mistake. Because they expected too much of marriage. Because emotions can get out of control when under pressure. Because love unattended soon takes a back seat. Because a successful marriage requires hard work, and a lot of people are born lazy or grow up lazy.

How have Sim and I managed to make it through more than thirty years? I can think of no single reason except perhaps that we each have an aversion to pretense and to everything implied by the word bullshit. We met young— she was a sixteen-year-old bridesmaid and I was a twenty-four-year-old usher at a wartime wedding in New York— but the bride and groom were both divorced and remarried by the time we got to our altar seven years later in Paris. And by then, having lived together for a time, and having considered other possibilities and other mates, we took the vows knowing we weren't embarking on a trip to the moon on gossamer wings.

And we were lucky in our lifestyle. Sim came along and helped out on a good many of my journalistic expeditions —including a two-month tour of the Near East and the Balkans with Adlai Stevenson. Back home, she joined me on a reportorial tour of the United States, labored with me in the local political vineyards (fortunately we were both Democrats), did her share and more of diplomacy as an ambassador's wife in Africa, and sustained me with care and devotion through some serious illnesses. Now, at fifty-four, she has her own business, so that we are both too busy to brood over whatever imperfections exist or have developed in our marriage. The major crises of this lifetime together have, I think, been surmounted, and while we both expect to growl at each other a few more times, neither of us need worry any more about getting bitten. We've made it through the badlands of middle age.

It's been work. Marriage is always work, especially when the partners are strong-willed and exacting. Without la-

bor—without a joint effort—love alone can seldom overcome the strains of living for years on end in close
association with another human being, not if he or she is
a whole person with a well-developed sense of identity—
in other words, an adult. And middle age, remember, is
when we are supposed to have reached adulthood.

What do I mean by work in respect to marriage? I
mean that you must make the effort to know yourself,
which involves owning up to all your faults and weaknesses. Otherwise you will never be able—or dare—to reveal
yourself to your mate, or really know him or her, or why
they respond to you in sometimes unexpected ways. Self-
knowledge is also a prerequisite to achieving the ability to
put yourself in someone else's shoes—which is the single
most valuable asset in marriage, or indeed in any human
relationship. And that's not easy, either. I mean also that
you must suppress the temptation to be overly critical;
we are all imperfect, and scolding a wife or husband for
some minor trangression is like blaming a hunchback for
his hump.

"To get along with human beings," said the French
writer Tristan Bernard, "do not ask them for what they
cannot give."

Don't ask a diffident wife to be the life of the party, nor
a clumsy husband to be an expert handyman. And don't
waste your time assigning blame or trying to change them,
especially after they reach middle age. What good does it
do to lay a guilt trip on someone you love? All you will
accomplish is to hurt them—and your marriage.

As for sex, I think the best you can hope for in middle
age is that your spouse smells good and doesn't get too
fat. Think of long-married comic strip characters like Dag-
wood and Blondie Bumstead in their double bed. All he

thinks about at night is getting up to make a sandwich while she sleeps through panel after panel, her back always turned to him. One reason the strip is so popular is that millions of middle-aged readers can readily identify with the Bumsteads. (We know she must wake up now and then.)

Exercising restraint, abiding by certain rules, checking certain impulses when anger wells up—all this is work. But every bit is worth it if your marriage is important to you, and your lifetime companion is more than just a casual friend. If not—call a divorce lawyer. And the best thing about marriage in middle age is that you come to appreciate the value of companionship, consideration, and continuity, just as you know that the full life to which most of us aspire must include marriage, however tumultuous it can sometimes appear.

We know that man-woman relationships are changing—for the better, I'm convinced—as women move away from dependency and, in midlife, find jobs and careers outside the home. There is still some truth in what Anne Louise de Stael wrote a generation ago: "Love is the whole history of a woman's life; it is only one episode in a man's." But only some truth. Today it has an old-fashioned sound. Men need love as much as women—need marriage too, I think—but the women I know no longer consider love "the whole history" of their lives. Is there a woman left like the nineteenth-century lady who learned Braille so that she could read at night without turning on the light and disturbing her husband? I doubt it.

A full life, I said, must include marriage—one is best, more can be troublesome. It should include children—never mind the drudgery, the worry and the grief they sometimes entail. These pass, for a number of reasons, and one of middle age's rewards, as we'll see, is that this is the time when parenthood gradually requires less and less effort and produces more and more satisfaction. It's also when grandparenthood, the best of all possible relationships, begins, for those of us who are very lucky.

6

CHILDREN

IN JOSEPH HELLER's novel, *Good As Gold,* the protagonist, who is about to leave his wife and family to move in with his mistress, has a lively exchange with his foxy twelve-year-old daughter:

> "You're moving out, ain't you?" she charged, with acumen rare in one so fresh in years.
>
> "No, I'm not." He made a face at the scornful laugh she discharged. "I'm merely packing things I'll need at my studio for my work and have to take with me to Washington."
>
> "Don't shit me," said Dina. "You're getting a divorce."
>
> "That's no way for a little girl to talk."

"Don't you care what happens to me?"

"No."

"Why'd you have me if you didn't want me?"

"Who knew it would be you?"

"What's that supposed to mean?"

"Ask somebody else."

"You really are the pits."

This passage is one of the best in the book, because the question, "Who knew it would be you?," echoes what is often thought and sometimes even expressed in parent-child dialogues when the impatience of middle age collides head-on with the harsh precocity of adolescence.

Impatience, tears, anger, exasperation—these are the standard emotions of parenthood, along with tenderness, pride and love. Why put the first four up front? Because, while prospective parents usually discount them (the birth rate would hit a new low if they knew what they were in for), these are the inevitable emotions of all the fathers and mothers who expect too much from their children and are consequently doomed to perennial disappointment.

There's no reason to be, especially in midlife, if we look at the whole balance sheet realistically. But this can be difficult, impossible actually, during these years when more or less amiable children metamorphose into teenagers. These are the years when it finally dawns on you that the offspring who were supposed to cement your marriage may in fact be breaking it up. Is there an American household other than the "Little House on the Prairie" where the overwhelming majority of marital disputes are not about the children?

These disputes are aggravated in middle age because this is when parents contemplate their resident adolescents and feel somehow cheated. Are these moody, unkempt, withdrawn, often unmanageable strangers their reward for years, decades even, of sacrifice? Of answering nocturnal crib sounds, processing mounds of diapers, coping with tantrums (we were once blacklisted by babysitters), attending dreary PTA meetings and endless Christmas pageants, hiding Easter eggs on rainy Saturday nights (I was eighteen years an Easter bunny), reading Dr. Seuss books over and over and over again, hearing things break, hearing screams, hearing tunes like "The Doggie in the Window" for weeks on end, leading chaotic expeditions to amusement (amusement!) parks, dealing with car sickness, air sickness and general sickness, losing the young ones altogether and organizing search parties over rocky beaches, up wooded hills and through unfamiliar airports, locating summer camps that normally turn out badly, and then, as the dating era begins, waiting for the sound of the tires on gravel, checking the clock and listening (if your child is female) for the interval between the car's arrival and the door finally slamming?

Some reward. Some return on investment. And the prospect then looms of deferring long-planned and richly deserved vacation trips in order to buy colleges for these ungrateful louts. This is the time when childless couples are briefly envied by many more parents than will admit it.

The concept of adolescence—that there should be a kind of hiatus between childhood and adulthood—is a relatively recent phenomenon. Until late in the last century, most young people went to work and got married soon after puberty. The word "teenager" didn't even exist when I was one. But now adolescence is here to stay, though it is generally regarded as an unpleasant time both for those who are going through it and for their elders who have to put up with them.

The idea of being sixteen sounds appealing when you're sixty until you think back to what it was like—the groping for identity, the upside-down values, the minor mortifications, the resented dependency, the peer pressures, the clumsy sex. And think back you must, in middle age, if you are ever to understand your sullen daughter or your silent son and avoid those futile, bruising battles that squander so much of your psychic and physical energy.

Generational conflicts, always smouldering, flared into open warfare in the late sixties, when most of us who are now middle-aged had adolescent children. This was when the parental authority whose outer limits we had seldom tested ourselves was now brazenly challenged by a misnamed counterculture fueled by drugs, protest rallies, rock festivals and disillusionment with post-Kennedy America. Long hair and casual sex became badges of defiance and "tune in, turn on, and drop out" a serious slogan. The Jefferson Airplane—slang for a split kitchen match that would hold a joint—became the name of a rock band. Some kids rioted and picketed, some got lost, some freaked out, a few O.D.'d. And all the overblown confusion was solemnly extolled in pop culture books like *The Greening of America* and drove far too many parents to distraction and despair.

Most of us lived more or less on the *qui vive*. Ringing phones sounded like alarm bells. At social gatherings, questions about children were asked only by those whose kids were—or who thought their kids were—doing well in school or college, active in athletics, neat, clean, "straight." The respondents squirmed: "Well, Sally's in New Mexico, taking a year off from school to work on an Indian reservation." A dead giveaway: the kid was probably shacked up in a cave on a diet of peyote. "Studying art in Marrakech" was another tip-off: hashish. "Bob's just fine; he's up in Vermont just now, working on a farm." Knowing smiles all around: the boy was either incarcerated or stoned out of his mind in a commune. Now and then a parent would admit to a juvenile problem—or report on another's problem with *hard* drugs; or the local weekly's police report (always avidly scanned) would list the names of those youths caught driving under the influence of controlled substances.

And then the parents of the teenagers who had not yet vanished or been expelled, arrested or committed, would feel a tingle of complacency and go on kidding themselves that Christopher had never heard of a toke or that Debbie was still a virgin. There were those who really did have such children, but they were well advised not to brag about them if they wanted to be invited again.

Our own family experience during this time was probably average, at least for suburban America. When we came home from Africa in 1966, just as the "youthquake," as one magazine called it, was getting under way out in Haight-Ashbury, Peter and Jan were fifteen and fourteen; Suzy, a latecomer after a couple of miscarriages, was almost three. For health and academic reasons, both the older ones had had to spend some time in American boarding schools while we were abroad, a circumstance which in subsequent family skirmishes invariably was produced as positive proof that we didn't want them around and were "trying to get rid" of them.

At any rate, Jan coasted blithely through schools, jobs, and marriages for the next dozen or so years, sustained by beauty, charm and wit; and her three-continent odyssey has fortunately left her still ebullient about life and its many-splendored possibilities.

Her capriciousness exasperated us at times. Why was she always acquiring admirers instead of skills? But on reflection I wonder if she would have been so different in any other decade. Probably not. The more I see of people from childhood to adulthood, the more inclined I am to the view that their basic personality traits are formed not by upbringing, not by parents and teachers, but by a biochemical process that takes place long before, perhaps in the mother's fallopian tubes. People can be guided, restrained, encouraged and helped to develop inherent qualities and skills, but I've seen no evidence they can be profoundly changed short of a lobotomy or a spiritual experience powerful enough to affect the circuitry or chemistry of their brains.

Our son Peter may have undergone such a transformation because he plunged into the teens more of a rebel than his sister. The reasons are complex, no one's fault and not pertinent to this book. It's enough to say he was difficult to manage and did not return affection readily, while today, as an adult, he is gentle and compassionate. He went to schools and left them; he lived in the Washington ghetto in the fiery spring that followed Martin Luther King's murder in 1968; he picketed and organized for Cesar Chavez, marched for the poor and was jailed in Washington. He hitchhiked across the country twice, at sixteen, handicapped by defective vision and lost glasses. When he called, it was generally to say he'd been arrested for suspected vagrancy. Between him and Jan, we had ample cause to lie awake at night in those years reassessing the rewards of parenthood.

Yet we managed always to keep in touch, to communicate, if sometimes only in anger, to assemble at holidays, and even to fit in some family expeditions between their own perilous explorations. Peter went skiing with Sim in Utah and horseback riding with me in Puerto Rico; Jan and I vacationed together in the Caribbean and

Morocco. Before, in Africa, we went on family safaris (Suzy saw her first wild elephant before she was one) and I rode a zebroid (a cross between a horse and a zebra) fifteen thousand feet up Mount Kenya with Jan and Peter. We drove through Europe, canoed in Maine, toured the Everglades, and snorkeled in the Indian Ocean. And much, much more, as they say in the commercials.

Why did we volunteer for so much family togetherness? In part because Sim and I thought it would be fun (it wasn't always) ; and in part because we sensed that storing up an assortment of shared experiences, whether pleasant or not, would in time give us the connective memories that we'd cherish when the storm and stress of adolescence had passed, along with the parent/child syndrome, and we would begin to regard and know our children more as longtime friends than as problems to be dealt with.

And that is pretty much what has happened. For example, Jan and I can laugh now (but not at the time) about the tribulations of finding stores that sold tampons on Saturdays in Grand Cayman, in Agadir and in Vilnius, Lithuania; Suzy can remember looking for amethysts with Sim in the wadis of the Draa valley, and being stranded with me at low tide on a coral reef spiky with sea urchins; and Peter can recall swimming with me in the Indian Ocean next to what we later learned was a deadly lionfish. All the shows and museums and movies you go to with the children are good input for the memory banks, too, but the outdoor things are best—the jointly tended vegetable garden, the savage croquet games on late summer afternoons, the wood stacked just an hour ago with Peter—now thirty—working the chain saw; best, because the recollection of things *done* together is always sharper than the recollection of things watched or heard. And outdoors is generally where the things that matter to kids are done.

Your last-born child, the one whose development coincides most nearly with your own middle age, is generally luckier than your first-born because of the dos and don'ts that most parents have learned along the way. When Suzy was born, I was already into middle age, at forty-five, and Sim, at thirty-seven, was close to it. As a result we may have avoided some of the futile frictions that troubled our family a decade earlier. The don'ts that will help you cope with children in middle age outnumber the dos—probably because young parents tend to do the wrong things more often than they fail to do the right things.

My own list, compiled in restrospect from the perspective of sixty-two, would stress these admonitions:

Don't expect too much from your children. Some win prizes, some don't. Some get into trouble with the law, some don't. There's not a hell of a lot you can do about it, so why make yourelf miserable wishing they'd been winners just so you could take part of the credit?

Don't worry too much about them; it just makes everybody nervous, interferes with your sleep, and, in moments of conflict, incites them to do certain things just to worry you. When I spotted Peter, at six, 100 feet up a tree, I knew I had a climber in the family and could only hope he'd get proficient enough at it so as not to fall and get hurt. When Jan, at eighteen, took off for an unknown destination in North Carolina with all her belongings in an old VW on a wet winter night, all we could do was hope she still remembered all the driving tips we'd taught her at thirteen. Accept the fact that teenagers have to explore the world beyond the perimeters of parental surveillance.

And be comforted that almost always, sooner or later, there'll be a reassuring phone call.

Don't complain about being deprived of those rituals regarded and even proclaimed as the legitimate rewards of middle-aged parenthood—the prideful high school and college graduations, the sparkling weddings and the candlelit christenings and bar mitzvahs, three generations deep. They happen—or they don't happen, and when they do the scene is seldom so idyllic as portrayed in the snapshots. Jan never graduated from any school except late and quietly, but while her first wedding was a slightly strained replay of the actual event, her second was everything the family of the bride could have wished for. Peter got out of the secondary school system via a state equivalency test, proceeded unobtrusively through two colleges, and got married without any of his family in attendance. We did watch Suzy, in cap and gown, receive her high school diploma, and the sun did shine and we took pictures. Adding it all up, I guess we did miss a few of those emotional milestones but perhaps appreciated all the more those we didn't miss, along with the good things that came later.

Don't demand respect, as a parent. Demand civility and insist on honesty. But respect is something you must earn—with kids as well as with adults.

Don't try to cast your children into a mold of your choosing. My father wanted me to be a Republican corporation lawyer and maneuvered me as far as voting for Willkie and attending law school for three months while I wrote magazine articles and made my plans to quit. I wish my children had gone to Princeton; I enjoyed my years there and I'd have enjoyed visiting them on that familiar campus in a nostalgic sort of way. But they didn't, not even Suzy, who had the credentials and the curiosity to visit the place. So it goes.

Don't raise hell about messy rooms; you'll actually miss the disorder soon enough when they're gone and their rooms are neat, empty and quiet, too quiet.

Don't threaten punishment of any kind unless you really mean to carry it out. Otherwise the threats become worse than ineffectual and only serve to trigger escalating verbal duels.

Don't reject your children, no matter what the provocation or how hard a time they've given you. (You never can, in your heart, anyway.) Don't close doors; alienated children are likely to walk in, their hostility spent, when you least expect them. Remember Robert Frost: "Home is the place where, when you have to go there, they have to let you in."

Don't give them money except in emergencies or for necessities—and never to win their favor or affection. Handouts mean dependency means resentment. At fifteen, Jan wanted a dollar for the movies and I could see a long summer of borrowed dollars and idleness ahead; so I gave her the classified ad section of the paper instead, and within a few days she was a mother's helper in New York making $35 a week and board. She wasn't happy about it at first; she was later. At sixteen, remember, almost any white kid with initiative can earn his or her own pocket money; a black kid has a harder time even with initiative.

Don't shield children from the consequences of their mistakes. Let them flunk for not working or be suspended for cheating; and let them learn that no one is going to protect them from the law if they're caught speeding, peddling drugs, or shoplifting. The sooner they learn about the real world, where there are no parents to help them beat a rap, the sooner they'll grow up.

Don't insist on expressed love. The chances are that your children love you more than they care to express. Just think back to how you felt about your own parents—and how often or seldom you showed them the affection they craved from you.

Don't feel guilty if your children turn out less well than you had reason to hope for. Their characters are formed very early; often, if you look around your extended family, you will recognize many of their traits in an aunt or cousin. Different genes produce different kinds of people that no amount of discipline or exhortation can change. I remember watching my three children reading on the porch of our summer cottage a few years ago: one had the Bible, one the *National Enquirer,* and one *Psychology Today.*

Don't rely on manuals or psychiatrists save in extreme cases. Chaim Ginnott's *Between Parent and Child* is an exception. ("The best book I ever read," said Suzy at age nine.) The shrinks are a mixed bag: some just charge you for common sense, others get between you and the child. Only a few, in my experience, have a sense of humor. One who did once told a mother who complained that her three-year-old son was insecure, "No wonder—wouldn't you be insecure if you were three feet tall, illiterate and flat broke?" The best therapist I've known was an Episcopal priest who conferred with Sim and me and Peter, who was then going through some serious early adult torment. After talking together for half an hour, we found that we were all holding hands and crying. Our tears, the evidence that we cared for and loved each other, was what Peter needed to see—and we have been much closer ever since.

Finally, don't ever underestimate your children. Their perception of truth, of the value of things, of what is honest and what isn't is often much sharper than it will ever be again; for age and experience tend to dilute our certainties just as they mellow our judgments. And since their obstinacy, even defiance, is usually a symptom of weakness, not of strength, your response, to be effective, must be compassionate as well as firm.

So much for the don'ts. As for what you should do, as a middle-aged parent of teenagers, to make it through these years with a minimum of lasting damage all around, here's what I've learned and am learning from long and continuing experience (Suzy just turned eighteen).

Enjoy the really good years—when your children are between four and twelve—as fully as you can. Spend time with them: the social and professional obligations that take you away are really much less important than they seem at the time. Don't impose your presence on children, but be available to do things with them; only later, for example, do you realize how sweet and wise and spontaneous a ten-year-old daughter can be—in ways she'll never be again.

Be honest with them always. They don't recognize or tolerate the gradations of the truth that we sometimes allow for in later life. In my notes on things worth remembering is a quote by a man named Davis—I didn't jot down his first name—who said, "With the young, the roughest leadership can be effective so long as it is nakedly honest." Let them down, and they'll never forgive you.

Keep your promises. "Next month," I said, "we'll build a cabin together that you can use as a clubhouse." A month later, Peter, age seven, said, "You didn't really mean it. I knew you didn't." That afternoon we started building the cabin.

Listen. Most parents are too full of answers to heed the

questions. "The fella that does all the talkin' ain't learnin' nothin'," said Artemus Ward. If you want to know what's bothering your children, really bothering them, listen a little. By a certain age they've heard all of your admonitions—they call them lectures—anyway.

Show care; offer love. When Peter was working in the Washington ghetto during the violence that followed the King and Robert Kennedy murders, we got a phone call that he was safe. But I went down there anyway. I remember walking past hostile black faces to the door of the Southern Christian Leadership Conference headquarters. I rang the bell. The door opened an inch or two: "What you want?"

"I want to see Peter Attwood."

"Who you?"

"His father."

"You Peter Attwood's *father?* Why come on in, man— you a *brother!*"

Peter knew I was worried but he needed to know I cared enough to come and make sure he was all right. You want affection from your children. Show some. You might not get it back right away, but the chances are that you will, in time.

Be natural; if you have reason to be angry, let it show. Children will forgive your outburst, but not if you suppress it. On their side, they learn eventually that verbal brickbats turn into boomerangs—just as adults learn that family fights are for the most part tension-relieving rituals that need not leave any scars nor sour the later years if certain conventions are observed—such as no trampling of egos.

Give advice, not repeatedly, but enough so that you won't get blamed later for failing to warn them about the consequences of wasting time, not acquiring certain skills, and generally lousing up their adolescent years. You don't have to—in fact must never—say "I told you so" later if they ignore your advice; they know damn well what you told them.

Be selfish at times. You don't have to put up with rudeness, puerile arrogance, or lack of consideration. Just make sure you resist being provoked into retaliation. The only effective response to an insufferable adolescent is indifference. And one advantage of middle age is that the emotional detachment which the practice of indifference requires is so much easier to achieve. (Gold, in the passage quoted early in this chapter, had even overachieved it.) You are more aware of your blood pressure so you allow yourself no more than a decisive bark or two. You have also learned that most passionate confrontations are transient and unimportant, so you have put away your sword and armor and can now sit in the stands and watch the sound and fury gradually subside in the arena.

To stay with the metaphor, I am not suggesting, obviously, that you leave the stadium. You can't. Blood relationships, no matter how we may deplore or neglect them, are not easily dissolved. What I am saying is that skirmishing with teenagers is a waste of everybody's time. For one thing, they are usually looking for certainties, absolutes, *answers;* but, with age, you have fewer pat answers to offer them. You can tell them what *not* to do, but this kind of advice is often scorned because it promises so little. And so withdrawal, to the bleachers if you will, becomes more attractive; either they will come and seek you out, or they won't. Just don't sweat it.

What else? Well, stay out of their way as much as possible, or they'll never mature, but be vigilant—for example, about things like drugs or the company they keep. Be a catcher in the rye, as defined by Holden Caulfield in

J. D. Salinger's 1951 novel: "I keep picturing all these little kids playing some game in this big field of rye and all. Thousands of little kids, and nobody's around—nobody big, I mean—except me. And I'm standing on the edge of some crazy cliff. What I have to do, I have to catch everybody if they start to go over the cliff—I mean if they're running and they don't look where they're going I have to come out from somewhere and *catch* them. . . ."

The time comes, soon enough, when you don't have to be there any more to catch them—when they finally grow up (although Leo Rosten has said that people don't grow up, they just grow taller).

Adolescence does pass, at any rate, and children in their early twenties can be good company. They even recover their sense of humor. Jan at twenty-two gave us a piece of pottery on which she'd inscribed, "Live long enough to avenge yourself by becoming a problem to your children." Together, you can look back on the strife and turmoil of the years gone by if not exactly with nostalgia then with understanding and perhaps some tacit repentance on both sides. Just remember they are now fully on their own and will resent your butting into their lives as much as you would in their place.

I said earlier that your children as young adults can become your friends, if you are lucky; not your closest friends—who would want or expect that?—but people with whom you can share confidences and generally relax. It's often best to see them individually, except at special holiday functions, if only because there's a tendency for everyone in a family to revert to their former roles once under the familiar roof. Brothers and sisters recall and resume old animosities and quarrels; a request from a parent is received like a command, or a parent will instinctively raise matters—like dress or hairstyles—that are no longer within his or her writ or bailiwick. And tension rises, tempers flare, and scenes from remembrance of things past are reenacted.

Reversion. After Jan's last divorce she stayed with us for a couple of weeks before moving into a new house. One day she went into New York saying she'd be back for dinner with Suzy and me; she didn't appear until 11:00 A.M. the next day. When I pointed out that a phone call would have been considerate, she became the teen-ager who had broken the rules. How could she call from—well, a man's apartment? I had to explain, patiently, that, at twenty-seven, she was free to spend her nights however she wanted without reporting to me; but as a house guest, she had an obligation to say she wouldn't be home. I think the message got through.

And if you're very lucky, you have grandchildren when you're still young enough to have fun together. Sometimes, hiking along familiar trails or working feverishly to shore up one more tide-threatened sand castle, you get a sense of quarter-century replay. But there's a difference: you're more relaxed, savoring the moment, feeling no sense of duty and not so concerned about things being done just right.

Grandparents in middle age are in general young in heart and bear little resemblance to the traditional or Norman Rockwell image. Not all have dentures and many play tennis and even ski. In some respects they are more playful and carefree than parents, perhaps because they feel freer—the concerns and worry that bedevil early adult-hood are behind them.

And the grandchildren are likely to be at their best, too; if they don't see the old folks too often they are never quite sure how much they can get away with, so they don't push. Thus, there's less need for scoldings, and so an easy harmony and spontaneous obedience often prevail. We should be so lucky? As onetime parents, we deserve no less.

Later on, beyond middle age, there comes a time, if you survive that long, when you'll need your children more than they need you—when you live from visit to visit, from phone call to phone call. My mother, at ninety-three, is there now. And I guess that's when you find out how much they do love you.

But that's another book, and this chapter has gone on long enough. If a conclusion is in order, I'd say it's better to have children than not. The grief and the pleasure balance out; but more than that, having children is a universal experience without which a life has got to be incomplete. And that is what I find saddest about those who miscall themselves "gay." As for childless couples who forgo adoption, it often happens that one, usually the woman, becomes a pseudo-parent to the other.

Just remember that when you have children, the chances are that their adolescence will coincide with the onset of your middle age. This should not deter you so long as you don't expect the experience to be exactly as advertised—or as described in those detailed annual reports of happy family activities that some people inflict, in the form of greeting cards, on their less fortunate friends during the Christmas season. It's better to expect nothing much but toil and trouble, and then the occasional loving moments come as splendid surprises and the shared adventures endure as precious memories.

There's perforce a generation gap between you and your children; none of you can forget the time when you were literally big and they were literally small. What is harder to accept in middle age is the realization that other younger people whom you grow to regard as contemporaries actually see you as a somewhat doddering old party who talks a lot about the past; useful, perhaps, for a job reference or career advice; occasionally surprising with insights about what the young agonize about, but still and all, definitely over the hill. If you sometimes forget you're middle-aged, it's never for very long; as we'll see, the young in growing numbers are there, always ready to remind you.

7

GENERATIONS

FOR MUCH OF OUR LIVES, we live in a world largely populated and for the most part dominated by people older
than we are. We may regard them with varying degrees
of resentment, awe, contempt and envy, but there they are,
making the rules and calling the shots.

In school, there's the college crowd, poised, assured, on
their way; in college, there are the prospective employers
waiting to be cajoled into giving us jobs. There are parents
and in-laws, always needing to be placated, and older
bosses whose approval can never be taken for granted. No
wonder that all through life, the character we normally
play in our dreams is usually no older than thirty, and
anxious.

Then middle age closes in, and all the old folks that have intimidated or bored us for so long are suddenly *hors de combat*—retired, gone away, senile, dead—and we find ourselves encircled by full-grown, even balding adults who can barely remember the Korean War, let alone *our* war—World War II. Their expressions, when not impatient, are often patronizing, for we have become in their eyes the almost old.

This is when it's important to keep communications open across the widening generation gap. Why important? Because there are lots of them and fewer of us; because our paths keep crossing and this should happen without strain; because we still have things to learn from each other; because the young and the middle-aged—all of us between puberty and senility—often have more in common than they suspect; and finally because to isolate ourselves, to associate only with our immediate contemporaries, is to consign ourselves to a lifetime sentence in the prison of senior citizenry, from which there is no escape, not even in a jogging suit.

Generation gaps are inevitable, as we've seen, with your own children. But communication of sorts is nearly always maintained because members of a family have shared too many experiences over the years ever to feel like strangers. (Enemies, perhaps; strangers, no.) Also, children grow accustomed to the gradual physical deterioration of their parents: the ravages of time that would identify you to the anonymous young as long past your prime make you only a slightly sagging mater- or paterfamilias to your kids.

To keep the lines of communication easy and open, we must recognize that there are real differences as well as imagined or perceived differences between the young and the middle-aged, and try to understand what they are. The first kind, which includes things like relative stamina and vitality, we have to live with; the second kind, which includes most of the stereotypes about age, are illusions that can usually be dispelled.

Let's consider the perceived differences first. They exist because to the young, almost everyone a few years ahead of them is old, except for a handful of show business celebrities like Robert Redford or Loretta Lynn. I remember at eighteen sharing a cabin on an ocean liner with our student tour guide, a thirty-three-year-old bachelor. He'd made a connection with a divorcée in first class and would sneak up there evenings, returning at dawn like a smug and lubricious tomcat. What annoyed me about him was not so much envy of his exploits—my own lustful ambitions were limited to surreptitious necking behind the lifeboats—as it was the fact that a man as old as he was should still be indulging in activities I associated with people in their twenties. Also, the word "divorcée" connoted a skinny dowager, therefore sexless, and old enough, as she probably was, to be my mother. But then, when I was thirty-five, I was just as surprised to hear some college students at a lecture wondering aloud why I' was identified on a book jacket as a "young reporter."

There can be no agreed-upon boundaries between youth and age. In your thirties, forty looks like the beginning of the end, which is fifty, and don't bother to talk about sixty. And yet the sexagenarians aren't doing too badly these days. I didn't vote for Reagan, but it pleases—almost rejuvenates—me to know that the occupant of the White House is once again older than I am, as presidents have been all my life until Jimmy Carter. And Reagan's cabinet is larded with my contemporaries who, whatever their shortcomings, don't *look* like burnt-out cases.

That's another generally (though often unwarrantedly)

perceived difference. It's hard for the young to believe that we can be as energetic and even as adventuresome about some things as they are. (Sometimes more so, because in some ways we're less inhibited.) The truth is that nobody changes all that much after attaining adulthood: we go through life with pretty much the same inventory of aspirations and fears that we started out with. But not realizing this, the young erroneously feel that we don't have much in common with them. Some are surprised, even vaguely offended, to learn that the elderly have sexual urges—and even satisfy them.

Another illusion about us that is prevalent among the young—another perceived difference—is that the middle-aged and the old are what they look like. They don't know that behind every aging face and body there's a relatively ageless person trapped there, not always trying to get out and generally more interesting company than the young might suspect from seeing the grotesque (to them) wrinkles, jowls and bifocals. Look at the eyes—not the skin around them but the eyes—of a once-beautiful woman and you can see that she's still there; believe me, she will not be boring to talk to. I didn't find this out until my own middle age; previously, like most men, I could not imagine having much in common with elderly women. I took it for granted that what had happened to them outwardly had happened inwardly as well. A cruise along the Adriatic coast, when I was forty-three, turned out to be an enlightening experience. Sim and I were the youngest adult guests on a yacht chartered by Agnes Meyer, the widow of the former owner of the *Washington Post*. The others—Adlai Stevenson, Alicia Patterson, the Earl Warrens, the Drew Pearsons, Clayton Fritchey, Mrs. Meyer herself at seventy-five—were all older than we were, and yet somehow as young, if not younger, in heart and spirit.

So you live and you get around and sometimes you do learn something.

Among other perceived differences that keep the young at bay is their belief that we are constantly judging them, whereas we in fact generally ignore their actions except when they harass, provoke or embarrass us. "You probably think I waste too much time and don't plan ahead," said the daughter of one of my friends. As a matter of fact, I did, but, as I told her, that was her problem and not mine to worry about.

No wonder middle age is still a time when fraternizing with the young is hard; for while we are all contempories, in the sense that we are momentarily resident on the planet at the same time, and all—from my ninety-three-year-old mother to my four-year-old granddaughter—exposed to the same perils, still the perceived differences between the young and the no-longer-young don't make communication across the ever-widening generation gap any easier.

In the summer of 1960, when Jack Kennedy was assembling a research and speechwriting team in Washington for the fall campaign, his staff had to turn to people who had worked in other campaigns—Stevensonians like me and even veteran wordsmiths like Sam Rosenman from the Truman and Roosevelt days. And I remember the subsurface strains that developed: the Kennedyites, in their early thirties, thought of us (late thirties, or early forties) as slightly out of date, just as we saw them as rather brash whiz kids. But where we did agree was in regarding the New Deal–Fair Deal old-timers—men in their fifties and even sixties—as superannuated nuisances, to be treated politely but not consulted seriously.

So much for the perceived, if illusory, differences between generations and even between age groups within a generation.

There are also some real differences between us—not just about who can play five sets of squash and who none— that derive quite simply from our having lived longer and seen more. Adlai Stevenson explained how this interferes with communication in a memorable speech he gave to the senior class at Princeton in 1954:

> What a man knows at fifty that he did not know at twenty is, for the most part, incommunicable. The laws, the aphorisms, the generalizations, the universal truths, the parables and the old saws—all of the observations about life which can be communicated handily in ready, verbal packages—are as well known to a man at twenty who has been attentive as to a man at fifty. He has been told them all, he has read them all, and he has probably repeated them all before he graduates from college; but he has not lived them all.
>
> What he knows at fifty that he did not know at twenty boils down to something like this: The knowledg he has acquired with age is not the knowledge of formulas, or forms of words, but of people, places, actions—a knowledge not gained by words but by touch, sight, sound, victories, failures, sleeplessness, devotion, love—the human experiences and emotions of this earth and of oneself and of other men; and perhaps, too, a little faith, and a little reverence for things you cannot see.

No doubt the students applauded the speech, but as a onetime Princeton senior who liked plain talk and mistrusted mushy concepts like "things you cannot see," I wouldn't have fully understood in my undergraduate days what he was trying to say. So many of the things we learn, or at least commit to memory, at school and college turn out to be excess baggage in journeying through life (what did Henri Bergson ever do for me?); indeed they sometimes have to be jettisoned, or unlearned, in order to avoid unnecessary confusion in young adulthood, to say nothing of middle age. It's a good rule to place in permanent storage in our memory banks only what we have been able to test against experience. As Emerson said, "The things taught in schools and colleges are not an education, but the means of education."

So Stevenson was right; most of the things we'd like to tell the young are incommunicable. I have taught classes at universities where uncertainties, no matter how fascinating, evoked only impatience in the class. But I could instantly get maximum attention simply by turning to the blackboard and chalking up a number of facts or assumptions in one-two-three order which the students could copy down for easy retrieval at exam time. Maybe what I wrote out for them was useful and accurate, maybe not. But this didn't concern them. Unlike Josh Billings, the nineteenth-century humorist, who said, "I'd rather be ignorant than know what ain't so," my students simply wanted to know whatever would help them pass the course. I'm not blaming them; the young fix their sights on short-term goals. Only later, as we acquire experience of the sort Stevenson alluded to, does the quest for knowledge or truth seem to have intrinsic value, clearly related to our own self-interest or to our constitutional right to pursue happiness.

So the fundamental difference between the young and us boils down to this, to use Stevenson's phrase: we've been around longer, so have had a chance to learn and unlearn a good many things they haven't really had any reason to think about.

There are a few other real differences worth noting if we want to maintain transgenerational communication. The young are more self-conscious: the younger you are the more you think that everyone is watching you, criticizing you, talking about you. The older you get, the more you can relax, knowing that very few people care what you do unless it's scandalous enough to be worth repeating. And it's relaxing, too, to know that other people are less interested in what impression you make on them than vice versa. But the young don't apprehend this, so they chatter a lot to camouflage their insecurity, or if very young, smoke cigarettes. As we get older we learn to say less and we find everybody enjoys it more—something that didn't dawn on me until my forties. Some of my middle-aged friends haven't caught on yet and never will, even though they seem to have progressively less to talk about.

But, as I said earlier, there are exceptions to every generalization you make about people. For example, I've been talking of the young and the not-so-young as if these were clearly defined demographic categories with common characteristics. But we know that some people seem to be born old (remember the kid in your grade school class who understood Einstein's theory and never played games?), while others manage to avoid growing up emotionally or intellectually. The latter go through life really believing that bigger is better, that nice guys finish last, that love conquers all, that the best things in life are free, that astrology is a science, that people who like animals can't be all bad, and that the check is in the mail. Read the headlines about UFOs, cancer cures and miracle diets in the supermarket weeklies like the *Star,* the *Globe* and the *National Enquirer,* and you may conclude that the average American housewife is a superstitious, overweight, gossipy, sexually frustrated hypochondriac with the mentality of a fourth grader. You'd be wrong. These papers are not aimed at the average but at the subaverage audience.

Digression enough: Let's dispose of the other real differences between the middle-aged and their juniors:

Younger people are more likely to think in a lateral rather than in a linear way. In other words, they may look at society and be critical of its shortcomings without regard to how much improvement there has been—for example, in race relations. This is because they have had no direct personal experience with the recent past. Sim and I can remember Atlanta in 1955 where we couldn't have a meal in public with some black friends, but 1955 is a year that belongs to the history books for people who are now as old as we were then. Not having witnessed those real but unheralded changes for the better that have taken place at home and abroad—particularly in human relations and international understanding—they are more likely than us to be pessimistic, even cynical. Vote? Why bother?

Another difference: We don't always laugh at the same things, or in the same way. It's been said the young laugh at the way things seem and the old at the way things are. I read that to mean that at a certain age you laugh at the antics of, say, Laurel and Hardy, but later on you laugh at the universal and familiar frustration that underlies their comedy. And I've become careful about telling stories; some work with younger people, some don't. Anecdotes about World War II—even good ones, like my being mistaken, in my bucket helmet, for a German paratrooper in Cape Town in 1942—just don't work; they're ancient history, as dull to them as my uncle's Civil War books, like *Frank Before Vicksburg*, were to me. Jewish humor, which is usually self-deprecating, even self-mocking (*"Nu, so life isn't like a fountain"*), is essentially middle-aged humor, and so I avoid telling Jewish jokes, even though they happen to be the best I know, to the young.

Bridging generation gaps requires some effort on both sides, like refraining from trying to impose music and dress styles on one another. We should be ourselves—neither overly deferential (or indifferent) on their side; and neither patronizing (nor artificially youthful) on ours. We must all recognize that some things, as Stevenson said, are incommunicable, and not even try to explain them. I will always remember two men who helped shape my life—one a teacher who valued good writing and one an editor who valued good reporting—because neither tried to lecture me or to insist that I understand what, in my late teens and early twenties, I could not be expected to.

"Some day," the teacher wrote on the margin of a short story for which he'd given me a C minus, "you will understand what I mean when I say that some day you will be embarrassed by this story." He was right. And four years later, as a reporter in the summer of 1941, covering a meeting of the local Lions club, I poured sophomoric scorn on their antics, for wasn't western civilization just then in mortal peril? The editor quietly spiked my story and simply said, "Some day you'll be glad I did." And of course he was right, too.

It's tempting to lecture the young from the podium of experience; but it serves no purpose and in fact only widens the distance between us. Of course we want to tell people in their twenties, even thirties, that most of their lives (soon about half) will be spent after the age of forty—and that what they do with the first third of their lives can mean the difference between enjoyment and boredom in the last third. Of course it's frustrating to see them making the same mistakes you did—wasting time, failing to develop new skills, giving up too easily. But you have to learn to say, what the hell, it's their life (unless they happen to be your own children who might blame you later for failing to shove them in the right direction).

Looking younger than your years can be both an advantage and a disadvantage in dealing with younger people. It's an asset should you feel compelled to give advice: if you look young enough they may listen to it since your opinions might not be totally obsolete. And it's a plus because, as a seemingly quasi contemporary, you may be spared that mixture of politeness and impatience, tinged with contempt, which the young often exhibit, usually unconsciously, in the presence of their elders. The disadvantage of looking a decade or so younger, as I do, is that more is expected of you—say, on the tennis court—than you sometimes feel like providing; you must also learn to put up with the pained expressions of those who discover for the first time how old you really are and react as if they had been deliberately deceived. The ritual complaint, "you look so young," really contains the tacit reprimand, "but you have no right to."

In short, to get along with younger people it's best to be natural, to ask questions as well as answer them, to act your age, to cater to none of their fads or follies, to care—really care—as much as many of them do about the future, to dwell as little as possible on the past, to display no more stamina than you actually have, and to confine your youthful fancies to your dreams—where nobody ever seems to get very old. It's even possible to become friends with the young —as I have, I think, with my daughter-in-law. And this is something you'll be grateful for later on should you happen to be among those destined for longevity. At eighty-five or ninety, with most of your contemporaries out of the picture, you'll treasure the companionship of youngsters of sixty-five or seventy. But the time to initiate and cultivate such friendships is when you are still middle-aged and they are truly young. It's not all that hard; just act your age.

And what about the very old—that is, those who look *back* on middle age as the golden years of youth? There are a lot of them and, God willing, we'll be swelling their numbers. I was at a party last year where everybody, to my amazement, was older than I and where I was jocularly assured that, at sixty, I was "just a kid." How do we deal with this group?

With the muddled—which means most people over ninety—just be more than generous with your patience; they aren't to blame for their confusion. With the others, be yourself, as with the young. Treating lively octogenarians with special deference is as gratuitous as treating a person in a wheelchair like an invalid. I often lunched with Robert Moses when he was in his eighties. Never did I feel I was with anyone but a cantankerous contemporary; nor, I suspect, did he.

But let's face it, dealing with the old isn't always so easy for the middle-aged. There's unexpressed resentment on both sides. Their physical deterioration is more advanced, but we less and less like hearing about it. They are thinking, "If only I were ten or fifteen years younger. . . ." And we are thinking, "My God, am I going to be like this in only ten or fifteen years?" And there's the shared knowledge we've both acquired from living a long time, includ-the realization that death is ineluctably approaching. And so, paradoxically, we have just a little too much in common with the old for easy communication. The very old and the young have no such problem. Since they have practically nothing in common, except perhaps their surnames, communication between them is for the most part wholly artificial—as well as loud, since the young suspect with good reason that the old are all deaf. Just listen some day to what passes for conversation during visiting hours at nursing homes.

And yet getting old, as I said a while back, isn't all bad, and getting along with people in other age groups doesn't have to be all that difficult. Not long ago, I came across a paragraph in a *New York Times* book review that seemed worth jotting down and which now provides me with some appropriate words for winding up this chapter about the younger, the older—and us.

> Aging is not simply decay; it is an accumulation of choices and consequences which, if there is any education at all, consists also of alternatives, an experience of strangeness, a sense of other possibilities, an appreciation of might-have-beens. Such an expanded repertoire, even though it exists only imaginatively, is not wholly ignoble, nor wholly useless. It is just more complicated, which is why the old should teach and the young should do.

And should you decide to teach, just remember not to talk too much (we all do) if you want them to listen.

8

WORK

SIGMUND FREUD once said that work was "man's strongest tie to reality." I don't happen to be one of his fans, but this statement makes good sense. Work is the best therapy for spells of depression, the quickest way of achieving identity and self-esteem, and the surest activity on which we can rely to justify and lend substance to our existence. That's why I believe that Descartes' famous principle, *Cogito, ergo sum*—I think, therefore I am—could be improved to read *Facio, ergo sum*—I do, therefore I am.

At no time is work more important to contentment than in middle age—especially work that has visible, tangible consequences, like building a toolshed, or measurable effects, like starting a new business venture. This is because middle age is when it has now become possible and tempting for some people to retire early; when the work one does at middle and upper management levels consists too often of processing the paper in the in-box so that it can be transferred to the out-box; when activity tapers off and you need to feel needed in your job—not merely tolerated because of your seniority; in short, when you want to affirm your existence and be able to assert, at the first intimations of twilight, *"ergo sum."*

Never mind that most of what we leave behind are sand castles destined for extinction; we still hope to leave our imprint on something, somewhere, however fleeting or trifling, as if to say, "Kilroy was here." It could be that we are all existentialists at heart.

Of course, not working can be corrosive at any age for most people, especially Americans. In the summer of 1945, I was sent back to Hawaii from Okinawa to teach a class of marines about capturing and handling Japanese prisoners. (We were due to invade the Japanese mainland on October 1.) Then the bomb was dropped, the war ended— but the class went on as if it had a bureaucratic momentum of its own. Finally we disbanded, but I was stranded on Oahu for weeks more, waiting for transportation home and sharing a bungalow on Waikiki beach with two other officers. Idyllic? Not at all. Enforced idleness never is. After four years in service, all we cared about was getting out, and getting a job.

I made it home on a crowded aircraft carrier in October and then spent four months looking for work, doing odd jobs, trying to write, going to noisy parties in Greenwich Village. Merle Miller wrote a novel, *That Winter,* about the restless, even desperate mood of so many of us veterans who didn't want to go back to school but couldn't find congenial employment. (The transition from company commander to shipping clerk could be difficult.) We wore veterans' lapel pins, called ruptured ducks, as proof we hadn't always been wastrels. And there was a lot of drinking, as well as a few crack-ups.

I was lucky. In February, the *New York Herald Tribune* hired me as an editor on the cable desk at sixty dollars a week. It was routine, sedentary work, processing overseas copy from 4:00 P.M. to midnight, but it was, at long last, *work*. And it restored my identity after months of being Captain Attwood (Ret.). "What are you doing, now that you're out of the army?" "Working at the Trib." For me, That Winter was over.

Aside from the need to pay the bills, what induces us to work? It's said Americans are still motivated by the puritan ethic, by the notion that idleness is sinful. Yet I've never felt driven by the threat of divine retribution. My principal motivation has been simply to avoid boredom, or more precisely that hollow feeling caused by protracted loafing—even by a day watching television from a sickbed. Unless I'm functioning—repairing something, writing something, or learning something—I feel restless and discontented in the evening. It doesn't have to be much; this afternoon, I went out with the chain saw to get some firewood, wrote two letters, read over some lecture notes, fixed the mailbox, and started this chapter. Enough for me to feel that I've paid my dues, so to speak, though nothing I did exacted a heavy price. In fact, I enjoyed some of it, like figuring out the instructions for assembling the grommets, washers, and screws that hold the mailbox, the nameplate, and the metal flag together.

Work can and should be fun; in middle age, it's fun that's work. The cruise ship passengers, the shepherded tourists, the Florida beach-cabana crowd, the residents of retirement playground villages—all, on close inspection, seem to be straining to prove that the best things in life, in the end, are games, sightseeing, and socializing.

At no age is this true. Among the elderly, the only ones who seem both vital and serene—and with whom I can feel contemporary—are those who are still working, or at least involved in activities that are more than just pastimes. This may be, as I suggested earlier, a peculiarly American attitude. I remember taking three months off in 1953 after a long and grueling assignment for *Look*. Sim and I took our two infant children to Mallorca, where for $100 a month, plus $14 for two servants, we were able to rent the grandest house in a seaside village. I did nothing but loaf, read, babysit and go for walks. Once a week we drove into the city of Palma where there were nearly always American tourists on the cafe terraces. When they'd ask what I was doing here, I learned to reply, "Writing a book." That was acceptable, even slightly prestigious. But if I said, "Nothing—just loafing," their manner instantly changed: I became, in their eyes, one of those oddball expatriates with whom they felt nothing in common.

But among the Mallorcans, my flagrant idleness, at thirty-four, was regarded with considerable respect. *"El señor no hace nada,"* I heard our cook tell a friend with pride. That I "did nothing" was to them a sign that I was one of life's winners, not to be scorned but envied and even admired.

What in fact do we mean by work? There is no single definition that would satisfy everybody. Basically, it's what people do to earn the money they need to live on. In early times, work was incessant: finding something to eat every day was a nonstop enterprise. Today, most people work not only because they want to live better than they would on welfare but also, however they may complain, because they want to. A few—mostly artists and writers but some businessmen as well, like CBS chairman Bill Paley, now seventy-eight, keep on working long after they've made all the money they'll ever need or want to leave behind.

My own definition of work is something that requires effort and makes a difference, however slight. Much work is humdrum, but if you ask the unemployed most of them will tell you that even a dull job is better than doing nothing. Working often takes a certain amount of will power, yet nothing that doesn't require some effort ever gives you much satisfaction. (This is why lazy people are generally discontented and why adolescents who avoid doing hard, unpleasant things often grow up without the psychic muscle they need to get through life; that, from what I've noticed, is the worst side effect of marijuana.)

Middle age is when the work we do assumes a special importance—for two reasons: first, we are still young enough to quit and do something more satisfying, as I emphasized a few chapters back; and second, we are old enough to be thinking about what to do with our heads and hands when retirement strikes. For instance, is your work something you can keep on doing, or would want to? If so, you're among the lucky ones. And if not, do you have a hobby or an avocation to replace your job—one that's more than just a recreational pastime?

If you have never considered work as something more than a means of making ends meet, then now is the time to start. Certain jobs are stultifying and strictly from hunger, like manning highway toll booths; others, that put some of your skills to use, can give you satisfaction over and above the paycheck; and still others, those that bring your essential talents into play, can be so exhilarating that you can't imagine living without such work to do. All successful creative artists have had this feeling, but so have a good many scientists, engineers, politicians, architects, businessmen and lawyers I have known. And for a few, their work includes the added reward of knowing that what they have created (or the difference they've made) will touch future generations. William Faulkner said it well: "The aim of the artist is to arrest motion, which is life. A hundred years later, a stranger looks at it, and it moves again."

Obviously, work that makes maximum use of your creative talents is best. Those who have the talent and can earn a living exercising it are the lucky few. But you don't have to be an artist—or a scientist advancing the frontiers of knowledge—to be creative in a fulfilling way. And in middle age, you have the advantage of knowing (or sensing) where your real talents lie—and where they don't —and being able to choose your work accordingly. For example, I found out by trial and error that I had some talent for editing copy and for communicating with and motivating people, but almost none for selling; that politics and diplomacy turned me on while financial statements and most of the natural sciences turned me off. So by middle age I was able to find more satisfaction in my working life than ever before, even though my final years on a full-time payroll included far too many hours of unproductive and repetitive meetings. But when you choose to accept a fat salary you must expect to perform certain corporate rituals: you walk the treadmill, or the plank.

The elements to look for in your working life as you move into middle age are variety, freedom of action, the stimulus of competition, and enough scope for what you've discovered over the years to be your real skills and interests. It's good to create something lasting, like Faulkner's artist, but the pleasure we get from our days on earth—at least a third of which are spent at work—has always seemed more important to me than the prospect of being remembered 100 years hence. I couldn't care less whether my home town celebrates my passing by naming a street after me. Functioning in the present with all systems go (all, anyway, that are still operative) is what really counts, and never mind whether posterity remembers you or not.

At *Newsday* we had more than 2000 employees working in a wide range of jobs. Morale was good, and always had been. At least a third of our employees had worked there more than ten years, a good many of them more than a quarter century. Why? In part, of course, because the pay and the benefits were good; but also because most of them felt personally involved in producing, selling and delivering a product we could all take pride in against lively competition from the *New York Times, New York Daily News* and the *Long Island Press*. Moreover, I tried to put people in jobs they could do best, which are nearly always the ones they enjoy most.

As for the work elements to look for that I cited earlier, our reporters enjoyed plenty of variety in their asssignments, and so did our ad sales staff: every sale planned and made, like every story researched and written, is a new and different experience. Circulation people were like the infantry, operating at the point of sale, targets of customers' complaints, exhorting and deploying some 9,500 carrier boys and girls, and responsible for getting a highly perishable product delivered on time to hundreds of thousands of homes every day. Production and clerical workers had less day-to-day variety, but with revolutionary changes in technology they were experimenting with new and more efficient ways of getting their work done. And the best of them could and did put their imagination to use. For example, our collating foreman, Walt Enderly, was in charge in 1972 of two machines called Sheridan stuffers that automatically assembled the several sections of the Sunday paper. But the television guide, which was less than tabloid size, often slipped out of the package before the paper reached the subscriber or the newsstand.

So Enderly improvised a contraption consisting of a coffee can, some kind of glue and a toothbrush which he attached to the machine in such a way that each television guide got a dab of paste to make it adhere to the collated color pack. People from all over the building came by to admire his invention. Improvising something like this is what gives special satisfaction to work that is normally routine.

And what Enderly did in production others did in sales or data processing or editorial or in what was called top management, where decisions, not all of them right, were debated and taken. (*That* was a good day—when you could say you made a decision.) And so not everybody in a company puts in a forty-hour week; the lucky ones whose work can also be fun—and there are a lot of them at any newspaper—are usually on the job or thinking about the job fifty or sixty hours, or more.

Thanks to my habit of changing jobs, I was able to decide early in middle age what my aptitudes were and what I got the most satisfaction from. I learned that there's no better feeling than tackling a difficult or boring task (after a period of procrastination and circling around it) and then getting it over with. The article written, the efficiency reports properly processed, the thank-you and condolence notes composed and mailed, the speech delivered, the photographs sorted and placed in the album, the garage cleaned out, the lawn furniture stashed in the basement, the term papers corrected, the car washed, the hair cut, the lawn mowed. The book started.

I've had another advantage. Most of the work I've done, and plan to do in the future, may have made and might make a small but enduring difference. What I mean is that so much of what people do does not make any difference, except in the short run. Indeed, most work has little intrinsic value other than keeping the wolf away. For example, I know executives who increase their sales volume and their company's profits, year in and year out, and of course this gives them satisfaction. Success at anything usually does. It can even give a perennial direction and meaning to life: exceed your yearly quota, surprise your superiors, be rewarded. And plan ahead so that next year's numbers will be even bigger. (This, too, I know from experience as a former participant in an executive incentive plan.) What's missing, unless you believe passionately in your product, is the sense of enduring achievement. For the net result, aside from providing the sales executive with the income required for a more comfortable life, has no lasting societal effects. In certain other professions, good journalism included, the work you do can leave people better informed or educated (therefore less likely to mess things up), ease pain and distress, prevent injustice, encourage talent, give pleasure, and at times even influence the course of history.

No, I'm not knocking good salesmen; I'm only saying that for some people, like me, work that does not leave its mark behind is just not enough.

One more word of caution about planning your work

life in middle age: do not be deceived or misled by titles. I've held a good many: chairman, president, vice-president, publisher, editor-in-chief, trustee, ambassador, special agent, commissioner, councilman, director, fellow, special adviser, professor—even doctor (of humane letters), governor (of a club) and secretary (of an art gallery whose president is Sim). The word of caution is that titles, while ego-nourishing, are meaningless in terms of job satisfaction unless they are functional as well as imposing. Publisher means something; so does ambassador (though much less in the jet age when Washington-based task forces take over in any crisis), and professor, if you're actually teaching a course at a university. But the rest can, as likely as not, be no more than inexpensive rewards for good behavior or for an anticipated contribution of time or money. Come to think of it, the only title I can associate in retrospect with work, period, is reporter.

Some jobs have titles that make them sound much more interesting, even glamorous, than they are; and by middle age you should be able to spot them as easily as you can the charitable organization that tries to appoint you vice-chairman of its annual gala in order to shame you into taking a table for ten. I had a friend in Paris who held the title of public relations director, Europe, for a major airline. From time to time he'd get profoundly depressed by the chicken shit (there is no better word) with which his days and many of his nights were occupied. One evening we managed to cheer him up; wasn't he, we pointed out, a kind of roving ambassador interpreting Europe to the VIPs who came his way, and by his own civilized presence in the city of light dispelling the ugly American image then prevalent among French intellectuals? By 10:00 P.M. he was smiling and buying a round of drinks; then came the phone call from his boss in New York telling him to

move his ass out to Orly airport on the double and find
Mrs. Darryl Zanuck's lost bottle of deodorant.

Not everyone, of course, gets restless in middle age
about the work he or she is doing. Without taking a poll,
I'd guess that more than half the respondents would express neutral or indifferent feelings about their jobs. Most
people I talk to look on work purely as a livelihood and
seek their satisfactions elsewhere. And indeed, most jobs
are dull; how can a bus driver, bank teller, assembly line
worker, short order cook, service station attendant, wait-
ress or file clerk—to name just a few occupations—look
forward eagerly to each weekday morning? Fortunately not
all people are activists, professionally, looking for challenges or stimulation in their work lives. Most are putting
in time, watching the clock and looking forward to the
coffee break, the evening, the weekend, the annual vacation and, ultimately, retirement, in that order. Automation
is rapidly reducing a good many routine jobs, but there'll
always be work to be done that will drive the doers to drink
or to hobbies—to bowling, fishing, woodworking, ham
radios, anything that blacks out the workplace.
    Those of us who have been lucky in our work—that is,
in doing for a salary what we'd want to do anyway—don't
often acquire hobbies. But in middle age it's advisable to
start cultivating a few for later on. Take up that long
neglected musical instrument again, or go to a watercolor
class and see if you've been missing something enjoyable.
Of course, you may have a vocation, like the poet Archibald MacLeish, that you can practice indefinitely, as he
has; but it's best to be prepared for the gradually widening
gaps in your days that will need to be filled with something
more nourishing to the brain and psyche than television
game shows or raking the lawn. Just make sure the hobby

you choose isn't something like weight lifting or scuba
diving that you might not relish after seventy.

I have a friend in his sixties whose favorite pastime for
years has been golf and whose extracurricular interest
before he retired was collecting old books. Now, with his
fourth divorce behind him, he leads a far pleasanter life
than most men his age by lecturing about the history of
golf, publishing a golf newsletter, and binding books—
a remunerative trade he picked up in the last few years.
He still travels a lot, most recently by sailboat across the
Atlantic, to ferret out rare books, plays golf in the low
eighties, and has graduated into late middle age with his
new identity established and his enjoyment of life intact.
It only takes a little advance planning, and good health.

Some people manage to reach middle age without devel-
oping any particular skill other than whatever they get
paid to do at their place of employment—pump gas, sort
mail, make change, wrap parcels, punch tickets, whatever.
They should acquire a skill, or convert a hobby into a
craft or profession before those last zestful years slide by.
The ability to do something interesting really well could
finally give them the self-confidence and inner security
they may have lacked all their lives and compensated for
with bravado and bluster. You may have noticed that people who don't like themselves are seldom likeable.

Women, now burdened with fewer children and free at
last to compete on equal terms in the job market, understand the importance of self-fulfillment. Take my wife, to
borrow a line from Henny Youngman; after dutiful service
as an ambassador's gracious hostess—as all wives were
described in State Department efficiency reports—and a
taste of corporate wifery while I was with Cowles, Sim
started a new and independent career at forty and is now
a realtor managing a fair-sized office and the owner-man-

ager of an art gallery and boutique. She also buys, reno-
vates and resells houses, does most of the housework and
family paperwork, gardens, entertains and skis. She doesn't
sleep late in the morning, but wouldn't want to; she found
out what she could do well on her own and outside the
home before it was too late.

My own experience—worth citing because it's the main
source, as I said at the outset, of my research—taught me
over the years what kind of work suits me and enabled me,
by sixty, to avoid work that doesn't. In school, I discovered
I could write fiction; in college, I discovered I didn't enjoy it as much as reporting. After the army I found out,
gradually, that I was also an editor and not bad at making
speeches (which used to terrify me). Later, I felt at ease
in diplomacy and learned that I enjoyed taking responsibility and making decisions. By the time I was well into
my forties I'd also concluded that there was no point in
pretending that I could ever feel comfortable in my skin
with figures, graphs, fund raising, selling, machinery or
financial reports any more than I could excel in school at
physics, math, most sports, and research that did not involve associating with other people.

And I'd learned, too, that it was necessary for me to do
something every day, however menial or trivial, that represented work—effort—in order to avoid being irritable by
nightfall.

Don't infer from this that I'm a workaholic. I know
them and have even ordered some who worked for me to
take the vacations they would brag about not having
taken—which I told them was an indication they were
badly organized executives. Workaholics don't delegate
jobs, never loaf and can't disconnect as I have done, increasingly, in middle age.

I took early retirement not because I was weary but in

part because I was getting stale. Budget meetings, planning sessions, industry conventions, corporate gatherings, company dinners and outings, ad sales presentations and community service ceremonies marched across the calendar, marking off the years with monotonous regularity. The big decisions affecting the future of the company had been made. And there were some areas of work activity I hadn't explored and probably never would if I stayed in harness until that milestone birthday when it's mandatory pasture time for all senior executives.

Teaching was something I knew I'd enjoy and I've been doing it, first at Long Island University, then at Yale, and lately as a visiting lecturer at colleges in the South and Midwest. It's satisfying, like this book, because it's a way of passing on to others something of what you've learned along the way. I also like politics; but my age and biochemistry—I need sleep and forget names—precluded me from running for any important office; so I got elected to my local town council and find satisfaction in knowing how things work and occasionally (as a minority Democrat) asking why they don't.

I serve on committees that seem worthwhile and appear to get things done, and have resigned from those that produce only speeches and reports. When I'm moved to write something, I know editors who'll usually print it. I try out new things—for example two weeks at an executive seminar of the Aspen Institute, reading and discussing books I hadn't opened since college. Not ever wanting to be a hired hand again, even an executive hired hand, I put some money and time into a magazine project which would have made me a part-owner had it succeeded. (It didn't.) So I keep busy. Every day. At my own pace.

I may be getting out in front of our tour group since the subject of retirement comes up later. It's well worth a chapter of its own in any examination of middle age because it can be either a traumatic or a liberating experience. Some people, of course, never contemplate the prospect of retiring. Irving Lazar, the legendary Hollywood agent, now seventy-four, is one. "The clue to longevity and happiness is primarily your work," he said recently. "It comes before your wife, before everything. It's a challenge, it's me against the world, and I've beaten them at it. If you keep moving, they ain't going to hit you. You won't get hit with a hunk of pie with a brick in it. If you stop, somebody is going to get you. I like people in action. People who stand still are liable to get run over by people like me."

Middle age is when some people do get run over by their contemporaries; or rather, when others run past them. If you've ever wanted to be a boss, this is the time of your life when you're most likely to get your chance. It's not everybody's bag—which is just as well considering how relatively few jobs there are where you can really feel in charge; and if it's not yours, you can skim or even skip the next chapter.

9

COMMAND

ONE DAY IN 1961, the State Department received a brief telegram from the United States embassy in Conakry, Guinea, saying, "Assumed charge 1730 April 22. Attwood." All it meant to the desk officer in Washington who read it was that I'd arrived where I'd been assigned. What it meant to me was that, for the first time in my forty-one years, I was the boss of an enterprise larger than an army platoon, a dozen writers, or a four-person office. I had suddenly become the old man for about fifty United States government employees, defender of the New Frontier and protector of the fate of several hundred American missionaries and teachers (and a couple of businessmen) in a tropical West African country the size of Oregon and written off, by most of the old hands at the department, as a Soviet satrapy now hopelessly down the drain.

Finding yourself in a position to give orders to a sizable number of men and women is something that usually happens to you, if ever, in middle age. In this era of giant corporations and instant communications, you will also have a boss or bosses to report to from time to time (unless you own the enterprise or occupy the White House), but on a day to day basis you can still find a satisfying degree of autonomy in a good many executive jobs.

An ambassadorship is one, as a few of us have found out. Running embassies, first in Guinea and then in Kenya, taught me things that helped me later on as I made my way up corporate ladders into executive jobs. That's why my initiation into diplomacy deserves a few paragraphs in this saga of middle age.

Guinea, as I mentioned earlier, was the country I chose when many of us who'd worked on the 1960 Kennedy campaign were offered jobs on the New Frontier. It was no political plum. ("You must have written lousy speeches to be sent to Guinea," said a friend.) And it did seem like an odd choice: a hardship post by any yardstick—hot, unhealthy, run-down, off the beaten track, and primitive even by African standards. But in the context of the cold war that I'd covered for so many years as a reporter, it was also interesting and important. When the French pulled out of Guinea in 1958, the Russians, along with every communist state except Albania, arrived in force with the aim of making Guinea a showcase for the Soviet road to development in newly independent Africa. Consequently, the country had become a lively arena for both intrigue and mischief. Furthermore, a third of the world's bauxite reserves are estimated to be in Guinea, and a Franco-American consortium was already processing some of it into alumina at an up-country plant and providing the government with what little foreign exchange it had. (The Soviets preferred barter agreements, which led to economic and political dependency.) Gaining access to Guinea's untapped bauxite resources therefore made the place important, certainly so far as the American aluminum industry was concerned. And Kennedy, particularly after the Bay of Pigs fiasco, liked the idea of our trying to eliminate what appeared to be a Soviet beachhead on the western tip of Africa. The situation, in brief, had most of the makings of best-selling fiction except for sex, drugs and glamour.

Morale at the American embassy was so low that I suspect almost any new boss would have been made welcome. Under Eisenhower, our African policy was essentially to support the European colonial powers (who happened to be our NATO allies), and since the French wanted to punish Guinea for choosing independence, we followed their lead. So the American community, such as it was, kept a low and passive profile on the Guinean scene while the Soviet presence proliferated.

Instinct told me that my first priority was to bear in mind Picasso's dictum that "the important thing is to create enthusiasm," while asserting my authority, as a political appointee, over career officers. No one else could do this for me: I was strictly on my own, except for the dutiful support of my deputy chief of mission, Tony Ross. Certainly no one in Washington was paying much attention to Guinea in the aftermath of the Bay of Pigs.

So I called a meeting of the embassy staff—about thirty in all—at Ross' palm-shaded, thatched-roof bungalow facing the Atlantic. While we had some drinks and the fruit bats darted about in the purple twilight, I could sense how they felt about me—resentful, as career officers naturally are, about anyone who makes it to the top of *their* profession via politics; curious—and also puzzled about why I had actually *chosen* Guinea; apprehensive—because ambassadors, as the president's personal representatives, have more arbitrary power than they sometimes realize; and maybe a little hopeful.

The meeting went well, maybe because we all knew it had to if we were to accomplish anything together. I told them I knew how they felt, that I needed their help, and that the president himself had an interest in our mission here (which was true enough but hard to believe in this ramshackle rampart of the New Frontier). I added that if anybody was really unhappy in Guinea I'd get him or her transferred without prejudice; meanwhile, I'd try to make living conditions more tolerable—such as increasing the fresh food shipments, showing an occasional movie, installing a Coke machine, and authorizing official travel to Dakar for dental treatment. (The only dentist in Conakry was a nonchalant Greek with a pedal-operated drill and no Novocaine.)

As a newcomer to the foreign service, I came to this malarial, neglected outpost with more advantages than most chiefs of mission. I had actually been to Guinea (for two days in 1947); I spoke French (the official language) better than anyone on the staff, as did Sim; and as a former reporter, I could write cleaner copy—or, in government parlance, draft better messages. Also I had, as they say, been around—around the world and even to the Soviet Union. Morever, as a political appointee with another career to return to, I could on occasion raise hell with the bureaucracy back home when that become necessary to get things done.

Moreover, I had a passing acquaintance with President Kennedy and could, in a pinch, bypass channels and get a message through to the White House. (It was a privilege to be used very sparingly.) The Guineans knew this, and it gave me easier access to President Sekou Toure.

Finally, the opportunity to exercise authority, always a delicate but essential initiation for a new executive, came that first night in the Ross bungalow when one embassy officer, a couple of drinks past the point of discretion, challenged my judgment (and the president's) that it was worth our making an effort in this avowedly Marxist country. This gave me a chance to adjourn the meeting and invite him to see me in the office in the morning.

Poor communications—phones were chronically out of order and our coded telegrams were transmitted via the chaotic Guinean post office—helped debureaucratize our job in that we could and often had to make decisions without asking and waiting for Washington's usually laborious and reluctant concurrence. (This enforced independence is something I would long for in later years as a chief executive on a corporate tether.) Once, my own concurrence in the appointment of a new AID director with no African experience or French fluency was requested in a telegram that didn't reach us until after the appointment was announced in Washington. Since I already had a good man running the AID mission, I suggested they simply withdraw the announcement. The resulting administrative turmoil back in Foggy Bottom didn't subside for a week, but I got my way, temporarily, in part because as a non-career ambassador I could risk being cantankerous in the interest of common sense. (Temporarily, because the AID man I favored was moved out soon after I left Guinea; the bureaucracy sometimes acquiesces but never forgets.)

A couple of years in Conakry was enough: we'd had to send the children away for reasons of health and schooling, and my assigned mission was accomplished. By 1963, the Russians were out of favor, the result of their own blunders as much as our diplomatic efforts: one of their ambassadors was expelled for subversive activity and they were even denied landing rights during the Cuban missile crisis at the airport they had built; negotiations for the development of the bauxite reserves by the West were under way; Guineans and Americans understood each other better.

And the experience had been both fun and rewarding to Sim and me, excluding the time out for polio. Diplomacy is one of the few professions in which husbands and wives can work in tandem, and she was good at winning the confidence and even affection of Africans. So when the chance came, later in 1963, to go to Kenya, we set out again, this time with less trepidation. The embassy was a good deal bigger—I was the old man now to more than 100 Americans, and there were some 2,500 American missionaries, teachers, businessmen, and even farmers scattered around the Texas-sized country. Visitors were more plentiful than in Guinea—ranging from Charles Lindbergh to Malcolm X—and the work more varied. We were involved in helping Kenya's economic development and political stability, and so I spent a lot of time on the road. And we had some lively moments, such as the riots and demonstrations that flared up after a force of Belgian paratroopers in United States planes freed hundreds of hostages—including United States diplomats—at Stanleyville in the Congo.

But all that and more is in another book. What is relevant to this one is that by 1966, when I left Kenya and the foreign service, I had discovered, at the age of forty-six, that I enjoyed responsibility and felt comfortable being in charge of things, motivating people, making decisions, and exercising authority. I'd also learned the rules of the games that are played—that have to be played—by those who deal in the commodity of power whether in their own interest or in order to get things accomplished.

In the government, the game is easy once you understand that the White House is *perceived* as the center of power even when its exercise of it is ineffectual. That's why I was advised early on by old friends in government to have at least one acquaintance working in the White House (it didn't much matter what he or she did) who would accept my phone calls. Most White House secretaries have (or had then) a "put through" list of a hundred or more names whose calls would not be shunted aside. Under Kennedy, I could get through to two aides; under Johnson, to three.

You retained the access by not abusing it; White House staffers get a lot of calls. It worked like this: one day I was attending an interagency committee meeting at the State Department to get approval to offer the Guineans help in building a simple (therefore workable) plant for producing palm oil from the nuts then rotting on the ground. I knew the president favored it as a practical gesture of support for a poor country. But the old-line bureaucrats around the table didn't like doing things for the first time, especially in Guinea, where the French hands-off policy was still in effect. A deadlock developed. So I picked up the phone, asked for the White House and, with everyone listening attentively, told one of my contacts that "the project the president was interested in" had run into snags at the department. Yes, I said, I'd let him know right away if we got hung up. And of course the power-sensitive committee swiftly gave the green light to the palm oil plant.

Games of this sort are not resented if you play them on behalf of a policy or program and not for your own advancement; in fact, you earn the respect of the professionals, as I was told I did by writing instructions to myself on a policy action (instead of waiting to receive them) and then taking them personally to the necessary dozen or so department officials for initialing *before* returning to my post—thus saving at least two months of needless delay.

Another example, this from the Johnson days: during the agitation in East Africa following the Stanleyville rescue operation (which had offended African sensibilities), I was recalled to Washington for consultation, along with our ambassadors to Tanzania and Uganda. Part of the reason was to create some speculation that the president was considering a more detached (i.e., less aid) policy in the area. But on our last day in Washington, we still hadn't seen Johnson: the Department had not been able to set up an appointment. And we all knew that only a picture of us conferring with the president would convince the African power structure that our consultation was serious.

So I called someone at the White House (something a career foreign service officer couldn't easily do), explained the problem and an hour later we went through a side entrance of the White House for a half-hour talk with the president and came away with enough photographs for the East African press to convince everybody that our Washington trip was truly a top-level exercise.

I left the government feeling differently about myself than I had when I joined it. I was still in my forties, that decade when most of us have an opportunity to decide whether we want to assume the burdens of responsibility (and the power that goes with it) or not, and I had had a chance to discover that I did. There are those who don't, or think they don't; they owe it to themselves to find out. For if you enjoy running things, no subordinate job will ever fully satisfy you; and if you don't enjoy running things, never accept a promotion, however tempting, that will propel you into a position where you have to, because you'll be almost sure to fail.

Now, in middle age, in what *Time* magazine in 1966 called "the command generation," is when your executive abilities are most likely to be tested—and should be tested. Now is when you are presumably adept at your job, know how to channel your energies, and, as *Time* put it, "to place Archimedes' lever in the exact spot that will shift the world a trifle closer to [your] heart's desire." And early middle age is the time when men and women who possess executive ability must be given a chance to exercise it before it's bleached out of them. I have seen this happen to talented victims of the rigid government seniority system; in the private sector, someone with executive ability is more likely to be recognized in time and moved to the head of the promotion line.

Actually, not many of us ever get a chance to run anything bigger than a department, a division, or a branch of a firm (except for those who own or operate small businesses). And of the few who do reach the top—chief executive officer is the one title that counts—not many can say they are truly the boss. Somewhere up in the corporate altitudes there is usually a supreme leader or board of directors with the power, normally exercised with discretion, to throw you off the back of the sled.

Back from Africa, I moved into a job with one boss, Gardner Cowles, who held a controlling interest in Cowles Communications, a conglomerate that included several magazines (*Look* was the flagship), newspapers, a book division, television and radio stations, and a newsletter, among other properties. As editor-in-chief of this recently assembled empire, I was supposed to see to it that our various publishing enterprises worked in concert, made money, and maintained an editorial quality that met Cowles' high standards.

I soon learned that a private corporate establishment differs from its government counterpart in two respects: there are somewhat fewer bureaucrats (people who keep a clean desk and don't make waves) and somewhat more maneuvering and conniving for status and power (though less, as I discovered later, than in the academic establishment). They used to tell a joke in Washington about a new game, like monopoly, that everybody was playing. It was called bureaucracy, and the only rule was that the first player who moved, lost. In the corporate world, there was more motion. And there is also more maneuvering for power because power is usually less structured and more diffuse, and the gamesman less hamstrung by a hierarchial system like the civil service.

I also learned that conglomerates don't command the loyalty they seem to yearn for. A smaller, less diversified company can because it is visible and does something— manufactures a product or renders a service. It is possible to feel a certain *esprit de corps* at Avis, where they can be seen trying harder against Hertz, as it was at *Look* when we competed against *Life,* or at *Newsday* when we competed against three rival newspapers. But who can feel like hitting the line for old ITT (which owns Avis), or CCI (which owned *Look*), or TM, the parent corporation of *Newsday?* They were invisible, except when platoons of corporate accountants came in periodically to check out the numbers.

As a corporate officer at Cowles, I understood how my presence at editorial planning conferences of our magazines could be regarded by the editors as intrusion. People in line jobs resent those in staff jobs; in the army, a major outranks a captain, but the captain commands a company while the major commands nothing unless he is filling in as a battalion commander for a lieutenant colonel.

So I was part of a corporate command structure at Cowles without actually being in charge of any component of the whole. I critiqued issues, proposed stories, sat on daises, spoke at meetings and conventions, and helped keep the advertising people off the editors' backs, but I was not actually managing anything, even when Cowles gave his blessing to something I suggested. Thus, when I was offered the job of president and publisher of *Newsday* in 1970, I felt the same sense of anticipation as when I first took charge of an embassy.

The corporate years had taught me a few things worth knowing if you plan to function effectively in the world of stock options, limousines and first-class air travel. To cite just three of them, remember that most top executives support you to the extent and for so long as they perceive you as someone who can be helpful to their own careers; don't waste time or energy playing corporate politics, but if you are forced into a joust, never forget that the person with the most proximity and access to the throne room always has the advantage; and let it be known, in a nice casual way, that you are always ready, willing, and able to leave in a showdown, especially one involving a matter of principle or your own authority.

By the time you reach middle age, there are a number of other things you should have learned (or had better learn) if you are going to be in charge of any activity in which a substantial number of people regard you as the boss.

First, delegate as much of your routine work as possible and give credit to those who do it. You must assume that your senior staff people are competent and treat them accordingly. Listen to them, borrow their ideas and blend them with your own. Remember Mrs. Roosevelt's answer to someone who asked her how the president found time to think up all the programs that comprised the New Deal. "But Franklin never thinks," she replied. "He just decides."

If your managers prove to be incompetent, or let you down, get rid of them. This is often the hardest part of a top executive job, unless you are sadistically inclined, for there is no kind way to kick somebody downstairs. To minimize the pain, be straightforward (no double talk), spare the victim's ego (no scorn, no anger), and make it fast (no twisting slowly in the wind).

Making decisions (such as whom to fire and whom to promote) is the most important function of a high-altitude job. People are called executives because they are supposed to execute, and are usually appointed to such posts because they have shown an inclination to do so. What the middle-aged executive has generally learned, however, is that the best decisions are the result of a kind of rolling consensus when your top aides are persuaded, one by one, that the decision you want to make is right. Giving orders is ego nourishing to some people, but if you want them carried out with enthusiasm you should, whenever possible, avoid issuing them. Real leadership is not making people do what you want; it is getting them to *want* to do it.

At *Newsday,* I could sense opposition to a relocation and reorganization of our circulation zone offices. So instead of ordering the change, the general manager and I took some extra time to allow the circulation manager (and his hierarchy) to modify the plan—not too much but just enough—so that it would be *theirs* and thus one to enlist their wholehearted support.

Second, you must be self-confident, which comes not so much from being smarter than those who work for you but from a profound, really undetectable and never expressed knowledge that hardly anything is too difficult to learn or so important that making a mistake is a disaster. Self-confidence means being able to say easily what for so many people are the two hardest phrases in the language— "I don't know" and "I was wrong"; and to respond to a foolish suggestion or request with a simple "no."

When I first joined the Times Mirror Corporation, I kept hearing the term "ROI" (shorthand for return on investment). After I asked a fellow executive what it meant, he told me he was astonished not so much at my ignorance as at my temerity in admitting it.

Self-confidence also helps keep you unperturbed in the midst of turmoil. It enables you to move your emotional switch to "cool" when tempers flare at staff meetings, or when the collating machines break down, as they did at the start of our first Sunday *Newsday* press run, or when the telegram that would dispatch the paratroopers to Stanleyville had to be sent to Washington.

Third, you must understand that once you have the power to affect other people's work lives—to promote, reward, dismiss, or transfer them—you can never be close friends with more than a very few of the most independent ones. So don't try; put yourself in their shoes and recall your own relations with your former bosses. And status makes no difference. I remember sitting in Ed Murrow's office in Washington in 1963 when he was director of the

United States Information Agency (and a few years before, more of a celebrity than Jack Kennedy). He pointed to a red phone on his desk. "That's the direct line to the White House," he said. "When it rings, I know it's the president calling. And I get the clangs, even though I know Jack pretty well."

"What are the clangs?" I asked.

"A rush of cold shit to the heart."

Fourth, knowing your power and the effect it has on others, you make it a rule to move around the premises; you periodically visit every department of the plant and you eat in the company cafeteria, wherever there's an empty seat. You don't talk too much, except to ask questions, knowing that what you say is likely to be repeated, distorted, and converted to gossip. You keep the old Turkish proverb in mind: A man is the prisoner of what he says and the master of what he does not say. But you should have two or three intimates among your top executives on whom you can try out new ideas and with whom you can relax and sound off.

Fifth, you shouldn't try to understand (or, worse, pretend to understand) all of the details of the various operations for which you are ultimately responsible; you need only to know what the computers do for productivity, not how to repair them or even communicate with them. The jargon of the trades and crafts under your supervision are worth learning, for you have to be able to talk shop with everybody, which means being at least conversant with what they are experts at. But as a top executive, your own expertise should be in coordinating activities that, without supervision, might be in conflict. Experts in a particular field are valuable but generalists are essential, which is why they are usually better paid. As Lord Salisbury once put it: "If you believe the doctors, nothing is wholesome;

if you believe the theologians, nothing is innocent; if you believe the soldiers, nothing is safe." And so running things also means blending and accommodating the views of various experts.

All this and more you should learn early in middle age—must have learned if you plan to spend your last working years in a position of leadership. And if your kingdom is a fief of a larger empire—in modern terms, the subsidiary of a corporation—then you must learn how to protect it from unnecessary imperial interference without appearing to challenge central authority. At *Newsday*, I sometimes felt like the president of an eastern European country who had to be careful not to offend the Kremlin while still retaining the support of his own people. So long as our bottom line looked good, I had no cause for concern about our independence; but I knew that a sudden erosion of profits would surely induce our corporate benefactors to give us the kind of advice the Russians gave the Czechs in 1968. And paradoxically, the more successful the subsidiary is as a "profit center," the more the parent corporation worries about it. When our revenues got above $100 million a year, one of my executives remarked to a corporate colleague that he was really having fun in his job. "You're a nine-figure company now," was the retort. "How can you talk about having *fun?*" And I recall being told, "You run *Newsday* as if you owned it." It sounded like a compliment at the time—if you own something you generally do your utmost to make it a success—but on reflection, I decided it was more likely veiled imperial criticism of vassal independence.

The basic executive skills, in short, are human rather than technical: judging people, identifying the phonies, knowing that insecurity plus ambition in a person spells trouble, sensing when you're being flattered or lied to, promoting the right people at the right time, and motivating all the people all the time. And acquiring through experience that aptitude best expressed by that wonderful German word *fingerspitzgefühl*—literally, fingertip feeling— that enables you to anticipate and respond to events. (For example, anyone with political *fingerspitzgefühl* could be virtually certain that Portugal would not go communist in 1975, that Somoza was done for in Nicaragua, and that John Anderson had no more chance of winning even one state in 1980 than Miss Piggy.)

There is one more executive skill that a surprising number of people at the top lack: the knack of knowing when they are being manipulated. In France, I knew an expert manipulator of American businessmen and enjoyed watching him in action. His technique was based on a few simple rules: Never answer a question quickly. When you do answer, use an illustrative anecdote, preferably one peopled with VIPs. Talk casually about large sums of money. Ask difficult questions about matters on which you know your interlocutor is very well informed. Grope for an English expression and when it is offered, come up with a better one. If the phone rings, pick up the receiver, pause, say "no," and hang up.

This chapter has been about running things, and, as I said at the outset, *should* be relevant to making it in middle age because this is when we usually get the opportunity. Or used to. For the truth is that there are now fewer and fewer people in our free enterprise system (and in government) who are encouraged or allowed to make management decisions without the approval of a board or committee. The current breed of executives are for the most part team players—and there's nothing wrong with that when one of them can call the signals without too much direction from the sidelines. Team playing is attractive to people who believe there is safety in numbers. But decisions made by teams or committees usually reflect the lowest common denominator of judgment or consensus, and the highest degree of caution. When news of Lindbergh's successful flight across the Atlantic in 1927 reached Emporia, Kansas, it is said that the telegraph editor of the *Gazette* dashed into William Allen White's office with his stop-press bulletin. The noted editor was interested but not as excited as might be expected.

"But he did it all alone!" exclaimed the telegraph editor. "One man—all by himself! Isn't that one hell of a story?"

"Of course it is," said White. "But alone, a man can do almost anything. Now if you'd told me a committee had flown the Atlantic, that *would* be a story."

And yet the trend in American boardrooms is toward a diffusion of power and responsibility. The larger a company becomes, the faster it gets taken over by the accountants, the lawyers, and the bottom liners who live in a world of reports, charts, graphs, projections and chalk talks. I sometimes wonder if the transcontinental railroad would have been built in 1869 had American capitalism been dominated by the no-risk mentality that prevails today. The audacious individual entrepreneur is an endangered species everywhere, except perhaps in the quick-buck fad market.

Corporations could, I think, tap and harness the energies of their best executives by setting goals for them and then leaving them alone with the understanding that if they don't meet the goals the first year they'd better have a damn good excuse, and if they fail the second year they would be expected to resign.

Most of us who like to run things would prefer such a

challenge to the now conventional system of being asked for status and progress reports every week or so. It's a little like being a marathon runner who has to stop at a pay phone every couple of miles to tell the folks at home that everything's okay. The best way for a company to make the most of its executives' talents is to get off their backs and encourage initiative; and the worst way is to give them responsibility and then treat them as if they couldn't be trusted to assume it.

Enough pontificating. What in fact are the advantages and disadvantages of being a boss? The biggest disadvantage is that you are never really off duty, at least in the professions I know best—journalism, diplomacy and politics. Everything you read and hear can be grist for your mill; at parties, you have one ear cocked for some fragment of information that might profitably be filed away in your memory bank.

The chief reward of running things is power—not the power to order others around, but the power to avoid being ordered around by others; not the power to win every game but the power to lose some and not have it matter. Power, in the final analysis, is freedom.

I recall a literal example of this in Poland in 1958. Sim and I were driving to the Baltic coast from Warsaw and stopped in a village to watch a wedding procession. We took some Polaroid pictures for the bride and groom, and a crowd quickly gathered. Ten minutes later we were in the police station, under detention for "blocking traffic." Our passports were confiscated and we weren't allowed to phone the American embassy. Finally I asked to be put through to the editor of *Tribuna Ludu*, Poland's Communist party newspaper, with whom we'd dined the night before. And then it dawned on the local police chief that we had . . . power; so we were promptly released with apologies, along with two young and very frightened Poles, to whom we'd given a lift.

Ten years later, my son Peter was also arrested—in Arizona. The charge was hitchhiking; the sentence, ten days on a work detail cleaning up the town in preparation for a rodeo. After a couple of days (he didn't mind the work but I didn't approve of slave labor), I called a friend in Phoenix whom I'd known in the government and who had some political clout. He had all the hitchhikers released within a few hours. Even in a free country, power can be useful.

But power doesn't necessarily make you famous. If fame is what you crave in middle age, you had better be in show business or big-time politics, which is getting to be the same thing. Celebrity status is rarely conferred on executives; you won't find many captains of industry featured in *People* magazine. The top brass at a television network may wield the power but the hired help who appear on the screen get the recognition.

As an ambassador, I was a third-degree celebrity for a few years in a couple of third world countries; so I had a small taste of what life is like on the real celebrity circuit. And I've known enough of them, thanks to journalism, to have seen the price of even a little fame, to appreciate its evanescence, and to understand why too much of it can be psychologically crippling. All of which leads us, as they used to say in the Rover Boys series, into the next chapter.

10

RECOGNITION

MOST OF US, whether we end up running things or not, live relatively anonymous lives and die without getting more than a one- or two-paragraph obit in the local weekly. Some of us like being unnoticed, or pretend we do, but just about all of us feel entitled to some recognition of our small successes, never mind the posthumous obit, by the time we reach middle age. For that is also assessment time, when wakeful nights are prolonged by nagging questions like: What have I really accomplished? Does any of it matter? And—does anybody care?

We all need a certain amount of recognition, especially from our peers. You don't have to be an actor or politician to be exhilarated by the roar of the crowd or even a ripple of applause. But while some are satisfied by the appreciation of friends and family, others require or hunger after more substantial reassurance in the form of titles, plaques, publicity, honorary degrees, and the conviction that somewhere, at any given time, someone must be talking about them.

This desire to be noticed, to be prominent, to stand out just a little from our contemporaries is what drives people to volunteer for worthy committees or perform civic chores or pay extra for dais seating at stultifying banquets. Their names and possibly pictures in a semicircle flanking the honored guest may appear in the next day's paper, even—who knows—on local television. If so, they can count on being greeted with a shade more deference by a head waiter at lunch tomorrow, even with a little grudging respect from normally surly offspring at home. This sort of thing can be reassuring to those for whom public recognition is evidence of their inner worth.

Most captains of industry don't, as I pointed out, have this satisfaction to the degree one might expect. Who knows the names that dominate America's economic power structure—the chief executive officers of *Fortune*'s list of the 500 largest companies? A David Rockefeller, yes, but only because a public relations genius named Ivy Lee got David's grandfather to burnish the family's image by handing out dimes half a century ago and made the name Rockefeller a household word. The others, no matter how rich or powerful, seldom appear with Johnny Carson or get written up in *People*. Everybody's heard of Barbara Walters, but how many know that her boss, the senior vice-president in charge of ABC News, is named Dick Wald?

There are different kinds of recognition, of course. One is to be recognized in the sense of being noticed, identified as a certified celebrity, and then often accosted in public places. If you want that, hire a good press agent, do something moderately outrageous, keep on doing it, go with the hype, and you just might end up as a television personality, like Zsa Zsa Gabor. Another form of recognition is being shown appreciation for something you've done.

Two illustrations from my own experience—one of being noticed, one of being appreciated—come to mind.

In 1952, in Paris, I was invited one afternoon by my boss, Mike Cowles, to join him, his wife, Fleur, and Ginger Rogers for dinner. (Sim was away at the time.) Like most American males who reached puberty in the thirties, I had been in love with Ginger Rogers, even while lusting after Betty Grable. But I managed to be composed, even nonchalant, through dinner. She was mercifully well preserved but not as bright and witty as I remembered her in *Top Hat*. Anyway, we pressed on to the Elephant Blanc, that year's place to be seen, and as we entered, the band leader recognized Ginger, stopped the music, and struck up "Begin the Beguine." A spotlight found us, dancers moved off the floor, applause broke out, and I assumed the role of Fred Astaire.

"This tune," I remarked, lurching into my box step, "must be very familiar to you."

"It isn't to you," said Ginger, and steered us expertly to our table while people stood on chairs to see who might be her new partner—or companion.

That is being noticed.

The other kind of recognition is a good deal more satisfying. When I left *Newsday* in 1979, more than 600 employees staged a surprise farewell party and vaudeville show for which I could barely find the words to thank them. I'd worked hard there and helped improve conditions for others who worked hard, but the appreciation, even affection, that was communicated that night was far beyond what I'd anticipated. (It was nice having my whole family there, along with a special friend who flew all the way from Los Angeles.) That kind of recognition is precious because it's the only kind that stays with you as long as you live.

There's something else, called fame, that some of us in middle age have aspired to, then glimpsed or tasted, and found wanting. (I'm using fame as shorthand for instant, widespread name recognition; you can be famous for nothing, like being Prince Charles, or for something transcending all ballyhoo, like Albert Einstein's $E = mc^2$.)

Fame is not necessarily linked to fortune, whatever Horatio Alger may have said, though having a lot of money certainly never prevented anybody from becoming famous. Fame takes work because it can be so transient (if you aren't a Lincoln or a Darwin). Where is Idi Amin these days, or Evel Knievel or Margaret Trudeau or Tiny Tim or Fanne Foxe? Has anybody seen Henry Kissinger or Bob Haldeman around now that they no longer wear the thick pelf of power? Or John Anderson, the candidate for president? They seem to have gone the way of Nehru jackets and the disco beat. (On the other hand, as we'll see later, once you are a 24-carat celebrity like Jackie Onassis or Truman Capote, you never fade away no matter how little you do to validate your status.)

But why am I seemingly digressing about fame and celebrities? How are they in any way relevant to the purpose of this book? They are relevant because I've met so many middle-aged people who strive in varying degrees and various ways for a moment in the limelight, and secretly envy those who are bathed in it; and because an accumulation of experiences has convinced me they are missing nothing—or very little. So if you are among them—if you yearn for a White House invitation, a choice table at "21," or seeing your name in boldface in the gossip columns— read on: you may be pleasantly disabused.

I have never been nor expect to be a celebrity. No one has ever asked me for an autograph, although once, arriving at a splashy social event in the wake of Raquel Welch, I was accosted by a mob of hyperkinetic teenagers.

"Are you important?" screamed a savage-looking nymphet.

"Not in the least," I replied.

"So drop dead, ya mother!"

Still, I have been a celebrity of sorts in far places where the sight of a United States ambassador with a flag on his car now and then turned a few heads. And I've traveled enough, both at home and abroad, as an aide to political heavyweights like Stevenson, Averell Harriman, and Jack Kennedy, to appreciate how much nervous and physical energy is expended by conspicuous public figures. (I've also noticed how quickly their batteries can be recharged by warm welcomes from large crowds.)

But for those of us lacking the special body chemistry that enables politicians to sparkle at breakfast rallies after three hours' sleep, being conspicuous is a strain that's only slightly mitigated when it's a part of your job. By part of the job I mean that, as an ambassador in Africa, I knew that people, both white and black, were watching me as they might watch old Uncle Sam himself, judging America by the way I acted and the things I said. So I made an effort to create a good impression among the white farmers at Nakuru or the village elders at Younkounkoun, and I enjoyed it; but it was still more of an effort than I'd want to undertake today, nearly twenty years later.

The only time that playing the part of Uncle Sam

bothered me was at the United Nations, where in 1963 I was a special advisor to our delegation and not often at center stage. But during one especially dull session of the General Assembly, I happened to be the only United States representative present. So when the presiding officer gave us the floor, I had to walk up to the marble podium and read from a piece of paper an aide had hastily thrust into my hand. The wording appeared unintelligible, but I started reading, hearing the sound of my own voice as from a distance: "The objective of my delegation in proposing the amendment contained in document A/L.445, is to clear up any possible misinterpretation of the fifth paragraph of the preamble and to make the language used in the fifth paragraph of the preamble consistent with that used in the sixth paragraph of the preamble and in the fifth operative paragraph. . . ."

And then, for the first time in memory, a sense of unreality and near panic swept over me, and I felt I might collapse right there in front of the television cameras and the world's assembled diplomats like a scarecrow. I rushed through the text in a daze and made my way back to my seat. "You spoke too fast," said the aide, "but I don't think anybody was listening."

For a journalist, there are also times when being conspicuous goes with the assignment. In 1955, Sim and I toured the country by car after spending most of the previous nine years abroad. We drove a white Austin Healey two-seater with wire wheels, red leather upholstery, and French license plates, a vehicle guaranteed to draw a crowd wherever we stopped. It broke the ice with normally reticent strangers (Where you from? How fast does it go? How much did it cost?) and led to a lot of wide-ranging conversation that eventually became the raw material of a book.

Three years later we explored eastern Europe, this time in a jumbo two-tone Ford station wagon. Many of the countries we visited—notably Rumania, Bulgaria, Czechoslovakia and Hungary—were then virtually off limits to American tourists, and we couldn't have attracted more attention had we traveled by UFO; again, being conspicuous was an asset in overcoming barriers of language, fear, shyness, and suspicion (Where you from? How fast does it go? How much does it cost?) These questions, too, led to more meaningful conversations out of earshot of the secret police.

Thus, being conspicuous can have its uses in certain professions: in journalism sometimes; in politics often; in show business always. Actors, for example, seldom move progressively up career ladders like, say, junior executives at Union Carbide. Actors can tumble down faster, farther and more frequently, and recognition by fans and critics are the main indices of where they stand professionally. They live, most of them, like the salesman, Willy Loman, in Arthur Miller's play "way out in the blue, riding on a smile and a shoeshine. And when they start not smiling back, that's an earthquake. . . ."

Frank Sinatra is now too solidly established ever to lose his celebrity franchise again even if he never sang another note. But when I first met him in 1953, in London, he was married to Ava Gardner and out of work. Even the shrieking bobby-soxers from the Paramount days ten years earlier seemed to have forgotten him. Ava, whom I'd once interviewed to her satisfaction, invited me over for a drink, and as we sat talking she called to Frank, who was in the next room, to get us refills. He was very much the dutiful butler. "Why don't you stay with us," she said, "and listen to Bill tell us about his trip." So he sat obediently in a corner and listened. Sinatra, listening. . . .

Then came *From Here to Eternity* and the glory days returned forever.

Celebrity status, once achieved by certain people, becomes a kind of club from which you can't resign. Fans, and the magazines that cater to them, won't let you, not when you have finally become an integral part of their vicarious (but no less precious) lives. But celebrities are not to be envied. Their psychiatrists will tell you that. I once spent an evening with Judy Garland during which she talked only about different kinds of pills and questioned me eagerly about the Swiss clinic I'd once gone to for exhaustion.

I've known others—my job at *Look* in the fifties made me an occasional tourist in celebrity country—and it struck me that not many, however rich or talented, seemed contented. "So few of these people have any calm centers to their lives," I was told by a Beverly Hills psychiatrist. "They're all on a high wire and not sure there's a net below them."

Being famous can also be a problem for temperamentally private people. It makes life difficult for the shy or the easily fatigued (people will accuse them of being haughty), and it cuts them off from a good many normal relationships outside their circle of fellow-traveling VIPs. For the celebrity game, as I've seen it played, is largely showbiz. One example: when Truman Capote gave a ball in New York in 1967 for Katharine Graham of the *Washington Post* and 400 of their closest friends, Sim and I were among the invited guests even though we had never met either Capote or Graham. We were there simply because Mike Cowles, who did know them, needed another couple to help host a pre-ball dinner party and got us on the list, which was printed in one—but only one—edition of the *New York Times*. (The list was yanked, I was told, after desperate protests from the uninvited.)

Celebrity status as measured by inclusion in such a list is really important only to three kinds of people: those on the make, destination undefined; those on the periphery of show business who feel their livelihood depends on visibility; and those whose egos require the reassurance of belonging to that shifting aristocracy that, in New York, can be found wintering at the front tables at Elaine's and summering in cottages around the Hamptons.

By middle age, if you've matured at all, you discover that you don't care to belong to any of these categories. You've also learned that titles are of no great importance, except to Washington hostesses and most Germans; that nobody remembers the people to whom statues have been erected in public parks, or even who was president 100 years ago (Arthur? Hayes? Cleveland?) ; that big tippers get faster service than Nobel prize winners and that nobody notices by-lines on articles except the writer and maybe his or her mother.

I luckily found out about by-lines long before middle age. In 1946, while serving as the lowliest reporter in the *New York Herald Tribune*'s Washington bureau, I wrote a Sunday piece on the plans under way to create the CIA. I knew a few good sources from my army intelligence days, and the Sunday editor liked it well enough to lead the second section with it—under my by-line. At noon that Sunday I ran into H. V. Kaltenborn, the dean of radio newscasters, at our tennis club.

"Bill," he said, "as a former intelligence officer, you ought to read this piece in today's Trib."

He pointed to my article. Was he putting me on? Not at all.

"And by the way," he added, "now that you're out of the service, are you still planning to go into journalism?"

Like everybody else, ever since, he had simply skipped the by-line.

Let's move on to the other kind of recognition, the kind you get not for who you are (or seem to be) but for what you have accomplished and how you have dealt with other people.

There's an element of fakery associated with this kind of recognition, too, and let's dispose of it first. Every noon and night in every city in America, banquet rooms are filled with overfed and overtired men and women gathered to honor one of their number or possibly a total stranger with a plaque, scroll, trophy, or other suitable artifact—and a speech. Whether deserved or not—and most recipients are not wholly undeserving—these affairs are normally a heavy trip for all concerned, though worse for the honored guests on the dais because of the heat and glare from the overhead lights and the difficulty of sneaking out early.

Awards nourish some egos, raise some money, and generate some publicity; but they are for the most part meaningless. In 1966, I received the moderately prestigious University of Southern California Journalism School's Distinguished Achievement Award of the Year although I had been back at *Look* for only three months and had done little except answer mail and read back issues. But my title of editor-in-chief and my magazine affiliation "balanced" the ticket of three recipients—the other two being newspaper and television executives.

Other awards I received while publisher of *Newsday* were tacitly and mutually understood to be gestures intended to cement the awarding organization's ties with the

newspaper and also (because the paper was often controversial and I was known as a lively speaker) a way to
help sell tickets to what were normally fund-raising functions. I attended these strenuous rituals because it was
part of the public relations aspect of my job as publisher,
but no organization ever got a break in the paper for
adding to my collection of useless trophies. (Plaques are
the worst—you can't even put peanuts or paper clips in
them.)

The most satisfying kind of recognition you can aspire
to—really the only kind that matters—is very personal and
rather limited. It consists of brief notes from both friends
and strangers saying how much they liked something
you've done. The notes can be quite short; one of my
favorite letters commenting on an article I wrote in 1955
on Jews in America came from a man in Brooklyn named
Moe Cohen and all it said was "Thanks!" Or the notes
can come in batches: whole classes of fifth graders have
written me over the years asking for a sequel to something I wrote in 1969 called *The Fairly Scary Adventure
Book.*

The best recognition consists also of things said sin-
cerely—like the pressman at *Newsday* telling me, when I
retired, how much it meant to him that I had once called
his home to congratulate him on the way he'd handled an
emergency repair job. And it's going back to places where
you've been employed and being greeted with real affection by people who used to work for you and with you.
It's teaching a seminar for a semester at Yale, as I did
last year, and at the close of the last class, being applauded
by your students. It's getting certain special awards—like
the framed certificate, signed by my fellow editors at *Look,*
saying, "We think you did the best job of foreign reporting
in 1958"; or the engraved silver tray I got from my

Princeton class at our twenty-fifth reunion. (It had never dawned on me until then that any but a handful of my classmates even knew my name.)

The recognition that really counts by the time you reach middle age is also, as I said, rather limited—in the sense that it need not involve a great many people. To be known (and, if you deserve it, appreciated) in your town or neighborhood is infinitely more satisfying than to be easily identified by the readers of *People* or to make the cover of *Newsweek*. When I go downtown on an errand, chances are that I'll run into half a dozen acquaintances, not counting the shopkeepers. Now that I serve on the town council, I'm getting to know even more people in this community where my elderly mother was born and still lives. I find it . . . well, comfortable to belong.

The sense of community, of belonging somewhere, is most important in childhood but also, as I am finding out, on the far side of three score—perhaps because in our impending loneliness we feel the urge to reach out beyond the steadily declining ranks of our contemporaries. That's part of the fun of being elected to local office; it's nice to know that some of your neighbors, at least, recognized your name on the ballot and may actually have gone to the trouble of splitting tickets to vote for you; and being a participant in the business of a town makes it seem like something more than a place to sleep and shop and pay taxes.

Jack Kennedy used to say he'd rather be first in Syracuse than second in Rome, and he never understood Chester Bowles, who refused an ambassadorship to Brazil in order to stick around Washington where by 1962 his future in the New Frontier was behind him. This puzzled the president. "Chet," he said, "would rather be thirty-second in Washington than first in Brasilia." I saw it Kennedy's way: playing an active role in local politics or running an embassy abroad can give you more satisfaction— and recognition—than scrambling for position among the gladiators in the clamorous federal arena. Having been from time to time a guest and associate of the famous and the celebrated, I've learned how much I value anonymity, even invisibility. Walking through a restaurant with a very visible friend, I've heard the whispers: "There's Lauren Bacall! But who's that with her?" But I can walk anywhere outside my home town and be completely unnoticed; and this is a pleasant, restful experience if you've been witness to the alternative. (What probably helps my invisible-man image is that I'm five feet eleven inches, weigh 165 pounds, dress conventionally, and have no really distinguishing features. As a detective, I'd be good at surveillance jobs—the subject I was tailing would never notice me.)

Retreating to smaller, more manageable surroundings doesn't mean that in middle age you shouldn't have a network of friends in Rome as well as Syracuse and indeed all over the empire. Life is easier when you're wired in to old pals in various professions and geographical locations. When my daughter was looking for a summer job, I called a geologist I'd met in Wichita years ago who now worked on an Indian reservation in Colorado, and he was helpful. When my math-major son got out of college, a new friend who ran the Long Island Lighting Company gave him a chance to prove himself with computers. Delayed in a mobbed airport at Rome en route to a holiday in Egypt, Sim, Suzy and I ran into Walter Cronkite, on his way to cover the first Begin-Sadat meeting. "Join my party," he said, "we'll probably get through faster." And of course we did, and made the plane.

By middle age, if you've lived a mobile and reasonably

inquisitive life, you should know scores of people from the different chapters of that life who'll gladly do you favors—and vice versa—with no quid pro quos offered or implied. You should, that is, if you've been a reliable friend to them whether their fortunes were up or down; if you've written notes on their behalf (because you felt like it) whenever they needed a recommendation or were unfairly criticized; if you've answered their phone calls and done your best to help them out with *their* problems; if you've managed to accomplish a few things yourself for which they respect you; and if you've always been honest with them whatever the circumstances or the nature of your relationship.

Nice guys (of both sexes) don't finish last, contrary to the old saw. They don't always finish first, either, perhaps because they lack the instinct for the jugular. But they make out pretty well, and one reason is they recognize each other and help each other out. There are networks of them in most professions (even among convicts) and for this all nice guys can be thankful.

So it all boils down to saying that the recognition we want the most is from people whose good opinion we value. Such people don't come in large numbers.

The best and most relaxing thing about late middle age is that you are under less and less pressure to strive after goals that you can now perceive to be illusory or unattainable. You are by this time accepted by your peers for what you are, warts and all. And you are free to devote the energies of your remaining years (never speculate about how many) to the things that you've discovered really matter in terms of self-satisfaction and recognition by others.

In France, soon after the war, I met a young man about my age who had been through three years of literal hell in a Nazi concentration camp. He had lost his family, he had been tortured, his health was damaged, his dreams had become nightmares. He had existed in a savage environment stripped down to essentials where only survival counted. And he had survived. But in the process his aspirations had become zero-based. And he had grown older than his years, much older. When I asked him one day what really mattered to him, what now kept him functioning, he answered without any hesitation.

"Le metier et les amis," he said. "My work and my friends."

I I

SECURITY

SECURITY IS ONE OF OUR most basic needs, according to
anthropologists, but it remains as unattainable for many
of us at any age as a burglarproof house. The best we can
hope for is to avoid panic. Your life insurance may be
paid up, your office filled with framed testimonials and
engraved trophies, your blood pressure normal, and your
seat belt fastened—but you are no stranger to moments of
apprehension and foreboding, not if you have an iota of
sensitivity or imagination.

And no wonder. This world we inhabit so fleetingly
under permanent sentence of death is a scary place if we
conceive of security as something more than beating in-
flation and investing in a sound retirement plan. Each

day brings us inexorably closer to death and the undiscovered country beyond, while pains and perils abound along the way—disabling illnesses, crushing bereavements, crippling accidents, and those midnight sweats when you wake up unexpectedly at what has been called "the hour of the wolf" and find yourself brooding about the human condition and your own physical deterioration, not to speak of nuclear stockpiles, acid rain and the depletion of the ozone layer. It's easy to see why people have always invented gods for supernatural reassurance and protection.

But aside from this generalized anxiety that afflicts just about everybody at one time or another, we also suffer three distinct but related varieties of insecurity—financial, physical and emotional; and for readers of this chapter, the good news is that all of them tend to subside, paradoxically, as we progress through middle age. Debilitation and death are closer, true enough, but by this time we have usually come to terms with the inevitable prospect. We've seen death take enough of our friends and contemporaries so that Mr. Thanatos seems less like a grim reaper than a benign and familiar timekeeper. You come to realize that dying, after all, leads at best to Nirvana, at worst to oblivion—unless you're cursed with a belief in hell fire and damnation, in which case you take care to say your prayers and behave yourself. So the stunning realization of one's own mortality, which hits so many people in their late thirties and early forties, usually abates as one moves onward.

As for financial, physical, and emotional security, these too are normally easier to achieve in our middle years.

When you are young and so long as you are poor, financial security seems all-important (so much so that it often mercifully eclipses all other forms of insecurity). People who have to worry about next month's rent and grocery money are understandably indifferent or even oblivious to the more esoteric fears that bedevil the well-to-do. By middle age, however, chances are that you have acquired some kind of nest egg or marketable skill, along with job security, and money worries no longer loom larger than life.

But while this can certainly relieve a good deal of tension, it comes as a surprise to some people that financial security alone does not bring with it the peace of mind they expected. In fact, relative affluence after a lifetime of making ends meet can bring with it a certain disillusionment: happiness turns out to require more than a paid-off mortgage. And so other suppressed or ignored insecurities, unrelated to keeping the wolf from the door, now make their appearance. (I live near a sanatorium where the steep weekly rates guarantee that the anxious, depressed, and alcoholic residents are very well-heeled.)

Still and all, the freedom from serious financial worries that can come with middle age must be counted as a big plus. If you and your spouse were the kind of young couple who strove to keep up with the Joneses, you're liberated: you *are* the Joneses. If you worried a lot about status, you should by this time have lost your fear of missing an occasional rung on the ladder of success. If you thought that money in the bank represented security, you should have learned with the passing years that the foundation of financial security depends much more on skills and talents than on titles and salaries which can generally be taken away as quickly as they are bestowed. My father, a victim of the 1929 crash, used to urge me, half-facetiously, to become a good piano player "because that will always get you a job in a high-class whorehouse." Well, today's massage parlors have piped-in stereo instead of pianists, but I'm glad *my* son works with computers simply because it's a trade that will guarantee him permanent job security in the radically new technological era now just getting under way.

As I said earlier about money: it doesn't necessarily give you more security but it does give you more freedom—to quit a dull job for a more interesting one, to explore the world if you feel like it, to indulge an occasional whim and never to be at the mercy of somebody else's whim. Big money, especially inherited big money, is something else—it can inhibit and hobble its custodians. For Scott Fitzgerald was right—the very rich are different, not just because they have more money but because they are, for the most part, so aware and protective of it—so fearful of invading capital, or even overtipping, so careful of a commodity that has sheltered them since birth, so soft and vulnerable under their lacquered surface, so patronizing yet wary of the not-so-rich, so clannish, so coldly gracious, so . . . out of touch with the world outside the high hedges of their estates and the portals of their clubs. No, I am not enamored of the very rich—I have known too many of them.

So much for financial security. There is also physical security. All of us now have it to a greater degree than at any time in human history; we live longer and suffer less, thanks to dramatic advances in medicine. And the world is on the whole safer to move around in—unless you happen to be a resident of Belfast, Beirut or the Bronx. By middle age, having survived illnesses, accidents, perhaps even a mugging, we tend like combat veterans to become fatalistic about what might (but usually doesn't) happen. Even chronic hypochondriacs adjust to the fact that our bodies wear out and develop funny noises, like used cars. As noted earlier, I've had more than my fair share of diseases; but, despite some lingering anxieties, I've learned not to listen to my heart beat, either literally or figuratively. (When you notice people surreptitiously taking their pulse, they are usually under 45.)

Those emotional allergies called phobias are something else, and harder to overcome. The United States Army cured me of paralyzing stage fright by forcing me to give lectures to entire regiments, and it also taught me how to fall (feet together, knees bent, elbows in, roll on impact); but not even parachute school could rid me of my fear of heights. Luckily, I never aspired to climb an alp.

Emotional security, the third variety cited above, is the hardest to achieve, yet the most vital to one's total well-being. The absence of it leads youth into destructive folly and drives their elders into depression and despair. Fortunately, by middle age, we've usually acquired the two essentials of emotional security: work that we enjoy and even excel at, and friends we can count on and—let's not hesitate to use the word—love.

Remember the young concentration camp alumnus in the last chapter, to whom only "my work and my friends" mattered; he had discovered the hard rock bottom of real life in the monstrous confines of a Nazi prison. But his words are equally valid in the more benevolent but often impersonal wasteland of modern urban and suburban society. For what we do, and who cares about us and what we do, are the things that will always matter most, wherever we are.

And once again, we who are middle-aged are much more likely to have built up the emotional scaffolding that enables us to look forward to whatever years we have left with the assurance that they will be less stressful than our early years—if only because fear of failure is less acute after you've been out on the playing field and scored a few goals; and also less lonely—because of the proliferation of family and friends who are normally supportive, for various reasons, of our emotional needs.

We know about family. The dutiful bonds (and anticipation of presents) that used to bring distant and seldom seen cousins to my Uncle Steve's house for his bibulous turkey-carving ceremony every Christmas have become looser now in families such as ours; but close-in relatives—children, parents, grandparents—still come when expected or summoned and are generally glad to see you when you go and visit them. If you get really sick, they turn up at the hospital and may even reveal by gesture or expression that they actually love you. For a good many uptight and undemonstrative Anglo-Saxon families like mine this is always a big emotional breakthrough, sometimes even worth the sickness if you recover.

Friends are more interesting, more volatile, in a way more precious than family if only because they are under no obligation to be pleasant, let alone affectionate. Unlike nieces and nephews, friends who drop by aren't discharging a familial duty; friends come to see you because they want to—not because they think they should. But who are the real ones? How do you identify those you can rely on—those whose friendship will endure long separations and different lifestyles? And how many will you still count as close friends by the time you're middle-aged and have begun shaking out the no longer useful business acquaintances and the summer soldiers?

You can answer these questions by asking others. Are you invariably glad to see him, or her? Do you always have things to say to each other? (Anatole France once wrote, "When I am talking with a friend, anything he says is interesting.") Do you feel you can say or do almost anything—display any emotion—and know your friend will understand and, if necessary, offer help, sympathy, advice, or simply attention? The questions are obviously rhetorical. With a friend, you never have to pretend to be calm when you're angry, or merry when you're not; if you don't feel able to relax and let it all hang out, then you aren't among real friends.

Friendships are built on shared experiences, either character-testing experiences or moments of pure fun. This may be one reason why friendships that endure into middle age and beyond are normally formed in our young adulthood, when we are more likely to get caught between the rock and the hard place, than in childhood, when we mostly play games. There are exceptions: some people's lives peaked in college or in World War II, and their friends remain those who were their companions in long-ago adventures. But for the most part, one's friends come from the ranks of one's fellow travelers over decades of successes, failures, laughter and love. Of my own close friends, only one dates from the thirties, seven from the forties, nine from the fifties, four from the sixties, and three from the seventies. I've made no new ones in the eighties, perhaps because it seems to be too much of an effort to get to know somebody that well anymore.

There were times and places in my generation that forged friendships among those of us who lived in them. Europe in the decade after World War II was one. We who worked there had a sense of vitality and excitement, of watching history in the making. The cold war was starting on a continent still partly devastated and recovering from a real war. As Americans, we were at center stage —needed, envied, sometimes resented, usually imitated. And as Henry Luce proclaimed, this was going to be "the American century."

In Paris, a bachelor like me could live pretty well on $100 a week. It was an easygoing city then. Girls were plentiful, lunches were leisurely, traffic was sparse; after midnight, the streets fell silent, the subways stopped running, and we walked home from late stints at the paper as though we were in a great quiet village.

Our bar was the California, across the street from the *New York Herald Tribune*. Teddy White was beginning to write his best sellers, and Art Buchwald his column. We reporters traveled a lot—to battered but bustling Germany, where cigarettes were hard currency; to London, where victory had brought austerity, and house guests from the continent were expected to bring steaks; to Italy, in chronic political and artistic turmoil—and to the bleak capitals behind the iron curtain, whenever we could wangle a visa.

On one of these forays—to the Leipzig fair in East Germany—Joe Alsop, who wrote a widely syndicated column that predicted doom with erudite relish, was the self-appointed dragoman of our caravan—which was a guarantee there'd be no dull moments. At Weimar, an off-limits Soviet army garrison town, he insisted on our stopping for dinner in the one civilian hotel—to the delighted consternation of the staff and clientele, who had not seen Americans in five years. Night life in Weimar consisted of the Soviet officer's club, which Joe, Don Cook of the *Herald Tribune,* and I invaded, armed only with a bottle of Scotch.

Our table soon filled up with inquisitive female guests. "Well!" boomed Joe, "the whores are leaving the Russians like fleas!" Next came a mousy East German bureaucrat named Dittmar who confessed to a thirst for whisky and English conversation. After ten minutes of listening to his defense of German communism, Joe declared, "Herr Dittmar, everything you've said so far is utter shit! Excuse me while I find the rest room, if there is one."

Two uniformed Russians with the blue headbands of the MVD on their caps suddenly barred his way. "Is possible," said one, "you go too far."

"You may be right," said Joe briskly. "It's long past our bedtime anyway."

We made our way back across a cobbled square to the hotel and waited in Joe's room for the expected knock on the door by the Soviet military police. Finally the knock came.

It was Dittmar, wondering if he might have a nightcap.

We left Weimar in the morning, unmolested, probably because Joe's self-assurance convinced the Russians that we must have had high-level permission to be there. But in Leipzig the police nabbed us, if only briefly, when I returned to our car from a picture-taking session with some *Frei Deutsche Jugend*—the wholly misnamed "Free German Youth."

Joe was reading a small volume of Herodotus in the back seat; he always traveled with some Greek history in his briefcase.

"I've had the most interesting half hour—" I began.

Joe gave me a look. "I dare say, dear boy, you will find the next half hour vastly more interesting."

That's when I noticed the man in the black raincoat and visored cap in the front seat. He held a gun pointed at Joe's chest. It swung around to mine. *"Ausweiss,"* he demanded, "passport."

So we were detained in *Volkspolizei* headquarters under a huge portrait of Stalin until my film was developed— fortunately all my shots were of grimacing youths rather than railroad stations—and were sent on our way back to West Berlin.

Memories of escapades like this are the mortar of friendship—like the incident in East Berlin (we seem to be stuck in Germany) when Dave Perlman, Allen Dreyfuss, Bob Kleiman, and I—reporters all—were arrested, again by the *Volkspolizei*—for gate-crashing a party rally. The communist thug in charge, an ex-Nazi with scars on his cheeks, looked at our press passes with pure delight as he read the names aloud. *"Vier Amerikaner und drei jüden,"* he chuckled. "Four Americans and three Jews." Then he ordered us out into the rain in the custody of a squad of tommy-gunners, from whom we were eventually rescued by a Russian colonel. That was one more happy and, for us, memorable ending. We all still keep in touch, thirty years later.

Perlman was one of three reporters I joined in a kind of cooperative freelance syndicate in 1950 that allowed us to roam around Europe, the Near East and Asia, writing stories about the cold war and assorted crises (which sold best in those nervous times), and also about offbeat people and places. In Cairo, researching a profile on King Farouk for *Life,* I found the pudgy and thoroughly dissolute monarch rather elusive; in fact he refused to see me. So I ambushed him one night in a cabaret where he'd gone to hear the newest addition to his unofficial harem, a twenty-year-old French singer. I managed to interview her at the bar; then, emboldened by two highballs, I walked up to Farouk. "Your Majesty—" I began, and in a flash I was ten feet away, arms pinioned behind me, and revolver nuzzling my rib cage.

One of the royal party, who recognized me, came over and had me released. "Lucky your hands weren't in your pockets," he said. "The bodyguards would have shot you. By the way, I think you'd better plan to leave Egypt tomorrow."

So I mailed my most important notes to a friend in Paris (the rest, as I expected, were confiscated) and pasted into a magazine the photograph of a sixteen-year-old girl Farouk had decided to marry despite the objections of her fiancé. Stan Swinton, who ran the Associated Press bureau in Cairo, had obtained the picture from him (the police had all three of us under surveillance) and wanted it smuggled out to his Rome office. So they body searched me and riffled through the magazine at the airport but never found the photograph. That was fun; and Stan and I, who have had a few other adventures in the intervening thirty-two years, are still good friends.

There are others to whom I'll always feel close—men and women Sim and I served with in the great tragicomic circus that was Africa; those I labored with congenially in political campaigns, in magazine conferences and in the news business—the kind of people who took their work seriously but not solemnly. For years I've kept up a zany correspondence with Art Buchwald, another satirical columnist named Bob Yoakum, and an expatriate adventurer (there is no other word to describe Jim Nolan). Why? Because the letters make us laugh. And because we're friends whose shared memories go back to postwar Paris.

Friends increase in number up until middle age, then level off, then start to dwindle. The casualty lists get longer; by your late fifties there's usually a familiar name on the obituary page every day. At my fortieth college reunion, a list of deceased classmates was unaccountably included in our weekend fun kit: 142 out of 657 starters.

Some friends you miss more than others; but in almost every case, death takes the only other witness to some remembered experience you have shared, and as the sole survivor, you are left just a little lonelier than before.

At the high noon of life, early in middle age, friends and acquaintances crowd and even clutter your days: the address book always needs new pages, the Christmas card list multiplies. But in the late afternoon, along about sixty, those of us old enough to remember growing up without television, air travel or polio vaccine begin to draw closer together as the twilight deepens, seeking, I don't know, companionship.

Loneliness, which is ever-present if latent for most of us, becomes more acute in these autumn years, rather as the air turns suddenly chill in September as soon as the sun goes down. This is when friends are most important—friends (other than family) you can call up at any time, day or night, long distance, reverse the charges, whatever, and be certain they will welcome your call. It's immensely comforting to know five or six such people because, wherever you are, you can be fairly certain of being able to reach at least one of them and escape that fearful solitude that may hit you unexpectedly in some hotel room in Kansas City or Singapore; or at home, alone.

I've discovered that not many of us can count more than a half dozen friends of this kind; most people I've talked to can think of only one or two. So it is indeed a lonely world, which is why the phone company's recent "reach out and touch someone" commercial was so effective. To the elderly, like my mother, a phone can be almost literally a lifeline—the one precious means of contact with her relatives and her few surviving friends.

And when friends are about to die—when you know

they are terminally ill—be sure to drop everything and go to them. You'll be sorry later if you don't.

I've been talking a lot about friends—what about enemies? Well, one advantage of age is that we tend to shed our enemies. Maintaining a feud just becomes too much of an effort. We come to realize that so-called enemies are simply people who let us down when we thought we could count on them: the harm they may have done you was almost always motivated by a desire to advance their own perceived self-interest, not to hurt yours. That's why I feel no particular animosity towards the few who have crossed or blocked my path. I simply avoid seeing them, even (or rather especially) those who were my friends. And that is characteristic of middle age: there are fewer people we really dislike—or like. Our feelings become neutralized. We understand, we tolerate, we make allowances for the flaws and failings of those we would once have regarded as enemies; we know that sustained anger can be a corrosive and stressful emotion.

And we can't be bothered with the marginals—the casual dinner partners encountered at parties who ask polite questions about families and careers and mutual acquaintances. Without being rude, we arrange to edge away. For example, I learned, years ago, to carry two drinks at social gatherings so that, when trapped, I can explain the second drink is intended for somebody across the room. All subterfuge is justified at this time of our lives, for time has become too precious to waste with strangers in the night.

The older you get the more you seek the companionship of friends who accept you, and the mood you're in, without question or reproach. Niccolo Machiavelli, a brilliant but lonely man, once wrote, "I laugh, and my laughter is

not within me; I burn, the burning is not seen outside."
If you ever find yourself acting like Machiavelli, get a new
set of friends or associates.

And what about the opposite sex? I think men and
women get along today more easily than ever before because there's a spreading assumption of equality in our
relationship that makes it as natural to be friends as lovers.
Sex intrudes now and then, when there's mutual physical
attraction, and can't be ignored; it must either be deliberately sublimated or made a part of the friendship. In
either case, the sexual aspect is never central to the friendship; if it is, what you have is something different—it may
be love, it may be lust, but you are no longer just pals.
A platonic friendship can be as satisfying in its own way
as a physical one (and often longer-lasting), just so long
as both parties feel easy and comfortable about it. I've
had seven or eight close women friends, and in only two
cases, both long ago, was sex an accompaniment to any
of these relationships.

I've dwelt at length on friendship because it is so essential an element in our unremitting quest for security and
for that stage just beyond, but much harder to reach,
called serenity.

Serenity requires a well-developed capacity for detachment so that when emotions heat up, you can quickly
switch your role from that of participant to spectator. It
takes practice, and not many people in our hustling contemporary society experience real serenity until they are
well into middle age. The knack of disengagement comes
fairly easily to those of us who have had heart attacks because our instinct for self-preservation tells us to avoid the
rush of adrenalin that accompanies anger. It's also easier
to cultivate if you've acquired the impregnable confidence
that comes from achieving your life's goals, including

financial security. In command jobs, it's what you're paid a high salary for, so you master the technique. I can remember, as an executive, how uninvolved I could feel in melodramatic, even noisy confrontations that now and then flared around me. I'd learned to live up to the old bit about keeping your head while all those around you are losing theirs; that's how you stay in charge.

And the ability to disconnect comes, too, from the knowledge, gradually acquired, that very little ever said or done by others can really damage you, leaving aside physical assaults. You can be reprimanded, insulted, denounced, or fired and still retain your self-esteem and that of others; even victims of torture develop a protective equanimity once they decide to endure the pain.

Deeply religious people display an ostensible serenity, but I find it strained because it usually needs to be constantly reinforced by rituals, Bible study, church attendance, and frequent prayer. I may be wrong, but their serenity strikes me as requiring a lot of effort.

You do pay a price for true serenity—for example, in discarded illusions that once fueled political and other passions. Detachment is not as much fun as being engaged in furious but often dubious battle; still, there's no hangover. Shrugging things off instead of hitting back—not getting mad, not even getting even—may at first seem somewhat . . . well, yielding, but serenity is not surrender; it's simply taking a strategic rather than a tactical view of everyday conflicts. A realistic view, too, which is also part of the price. For some, it can be profoundly disillusioning to realize that no one cares very much about you—unless you're in their way or can help them *on* their way.

But the wisdom acquired with age also has its rewards: you don't buy trouble, for one thing. The father of one of my friends had a favorite saying: "Once I was young, now I am old. I've had many troubles, most of which never happened."

Security; serenity. Suppose I look around and see where my own head is at, to borrow a phrase from the sixties.

At this moment, I am sitting in the sunshine on the back deck of my home in Connecticut, writing these words on a yellow pad, while my arthritic old Yorkie, Ratzo, dreams of chicken parts and puppyhood in the shade of my chair. It's quiet: I hear the drone of a plane, the buzzing of a distant moped, the faint noise of rock music from the young house painter's radio next door. (Why can't youth tolerate silence?) And there are the small sounds of ripening summer—rustling foliage, murmuring bees, bird calls.

My thirty-first wedding anniversary is imminent. Sim and I get along about as well as we did at all our others; we quarrel and we make up. I'll take her out for dinner, I'm not sure where. Suzy is at our Block Island house, reading Shakespeare and banding migrating birds with other ornithologists. Jan's in New York, working on the periphery of the theater, twice-divorced at twenty-eight, getting along. Peter's at his computer job; he's coming over for dinner tonight with my mother, still pretty spry at ninety-three. In a couple of weeks, his kids will be arriving from Pittsburgh for a long visit by the ocean.

I have a slight headache, the result of attending that Princeton reunion. Most of my classmates looked depressingly old, as usual. Thirty of them, probably the fat ones and the smokers, died in the past five years, almost as many as we lost in World War II. Next weekend will be quieter: I'll be visiting old friends in northern Connecticut (Sim and I introduced them in Paris in 1952) and, with a surveyor, walking the boundary of some farmland we bought; we'll get in some tennis and poker, maybe a few holes of golf.

I notice the hedge needs clipping and remember that I forgot to spray the trees. Ratzo is asking for his supper. There's some mail to be answered, and a short piece for *Newsday* I want to write about Reagan—an idea came to me in the night.

Soon this chapter will be done and I'll celebrate with a gin and tonic and a swim in the pool. Maybe I can work in a nap before Sim gets home from her real estate office.

So, am I secure? Sure; why shouldn't I be? No major money or family problems. A good many close friends. A little apprehension now and then, like everybody who's been sick and gets occasional reminders, such as chest pains on that steep fourteenth hole. But no fear.

Am I serene? I suppose so. I know who I am and am friends with myself. But of course I have restless moments. So, to sum up, put it this way: I am just serene enough not to be upset by small calamities (or their prospect); but not so serene, thank God, as to be any less indignant than I have ever been about the stupidity and inhumanity of the wider world in which I've always felt the need to play some part; and now, at sixty-two and in retirement, still do.

12

RETIREMENT

THE TROUBLE WITH the word "retirement" is that it has connotations of retreat. (The French word for retirement—*retraite*—even sounds like it.) That's why some middle-aged people who either choose or are obliged to retire from a job can easily feel defeated. They needn't. Retirement at best is a fresh start, possibly an escape from a dull routine; and, at worst, a change of pace.

Once you get over the adolescent feeling that people are always judging you, then you don't have to feel ill at ease about no longer being in the rat race or the conventional work force. You can even celebrate your liberation. But it takes both preparation and practice. How to go about it, based on my nearly three-year experience as a retiree, is the purpose of this chapter.

It's well to remember at the outset that the only people likely to be bothered by *your* loss of a clearly identifiable identity are hostesses at elegant dinner parties. The guests they like best of all are those they can introduce as, "Of course you know Jacqueline Onassis," with "Have you met Senator Baker?" next in order of preference. Then comes "Let me introduce you to Dr. Wexler—he's a psychiatrist." (Psychiatrist is better than dentist.) And at the bottom of the list is "This is Mr. Attwood. He used to be in journalism." Fortunately, since my retirement, I get invited to far fewer fashionable parties. What now protects me and my ilk is a lack of suitable identity that will add luster to the gathering.

For those of you reading this who are contemplating retirement and don't want to feel completely out of it, some warnings, observations, suggestions and conclusions, most of them reassuring, are now in order from your self-appointed guide through these midlife mazes. I realize that this chapter applies more to men than to women, but not as much as it would have twenty years ago. Working women reach retirement age, too; and non-career housewives are affected in a variety of ways by the impact of retirement on their husbands.

First, the warnings: the initial few months in civvies, so to speak, are the hardest. I use the civvies metaphor because I can recall my deflating transition in 1945 from beribboned Captain Attwood—no problem getting a good table, never mind the tip—to Mr. Attwood, unemployed, veteran's pin in the lapel of his prewar suit, not otherwise classifiable. For the identity problem in America is as important today, at least in my generation, as it was then. In this society, you are very often what your job is. So be prepared for blank stares or even embarrassed silence when you are revealed to be without affiliation.

The worst thing you can do is to defer the moment of truth by clinging to a job for which you no longer have either the zeal or the energy. That's like being an aging boxer still defending his title when he knows his legs won't carry him beyond seven rounds. Kidding yourself is always a mistake but never more so than in middle age, when the fact must be faced that after fifty, or even forty, you just don't have the energy once taken for granted. That's why, in my profession, the best reporters—not the wisest but the best—are usually younger than forty. You often have to keep going a few extra miles, or hours, to uncover the hidden, illuminating element that can transform a collection of facts into a coherent story. A reporter of fifty or sixty can substitute hunches for leg work and get away with it some of the time; but not all of the time, which is why the young should report and their elders should edit.

The problems of retirement afflict both the retiree and the people he or she associates with. Unless you look convincingly old, notice how their expressions change to puzzlement and uncertainty when they discover you're "retired." It's as if you'd suddenly lost thirty pounds; they figure something might be wrong, and hesitate to ask more. And it's no fun disappointing people by being nobody except a former something. Never mind the ones to whom you've been important as an ornament or as a useful contact because of your position in whatever power structure you operated in. Good riddance to them. But the nice folks who ask with unfeigned interest, "What do you do?" should not be made to feel ill at ease. To answer, "Nothing," is rude and probably also inaccurate even if all you do is read comic books and play backgammon.

And to answer, "I'm retired," is somehow not enough; it begs the question, "Why?" And to answer by listing in detail all of your various postretirement activities (such as serving on the school board, learning the zither or playing the horses) is both embarrassing and boring to your interlocutor. So I think the best answer is to say, "I'm writing a book."

The advantage of this reply is that, to most people, writing is a mysterious but eminently respectable activity. Also, the answer requires no elaboration: to the rare questioner who asks what the book is about, a quiet smile and a murmured, "I'd rather not talk about it until it's done," will end the discussion gracefully. The only drawback is that it may not sound entirely plausible if you're known to have been a lifelong certified public accountant, say, or a beautician without any literary aspirations. (It *could* be a textbook or anthology of gossip, of course.) But if you've ever written anything at all for publication, you can generally use the book dodge for the rest of your life without ever producing a single galley proof. "How's the book going?" someone might ask on the ninth tee three years hence. "Coming along fine," you say. "About ready to start editing and polishing." And you drive off.

Another retirement problem, which doesn't last long, is the feeling of being an outsider at events in which you used to play some part. For example, I enjoy political conventions and have attended seven or eight since 1952, either as a reporter, a speech writer or a news executive checking up on the troops. Anyway, I always rated a badge and floor pass. But in New York in 1980, after leaving *Newsday*, I only went to a couple of the many peripheral parties; and even there, even among old friends, I realized that I now and for the first time lacked those intangible insider credentials that make the difference between really belonging and just being present. So I watched the rest of the convention proceedings on television and discovered to my satisfaction that I really didn't miss the old familiar frenzy anymore. I'd been there.

A symptom of middle age? Of course. For this is when you learn, if you haven't before, that there is a time for doing certain kinds of things, and a time to stop doing them; and that stopping shouldn't be confused with giving up or retreating or even slowing down.

Still another retirement problem is fending off the onslaught of program chairpersons looking for speakers, and old acquaintances bent on recruiting you for worthwhile committees. When employed, you can always plead the pressure of business or schedule mythical trips to the West Coast. But as a known retiree, your availability is taken for granted and excuses are harder to manufacture. (In fact, you might have been asked to give the speech because the group's first choice pleaded the pressure of business.) The best defense against speaking engagements is probably to sign up with a lecture bureau to which you can refer all requests; this works because not many organizations are likely to want you badly enough to pay a fee. As for joining committees, just tell them candidly you are already overcommitted and don't feel that, in good conscience, you should take on additional responsibilities to which you couldn't devote your best efforts. (The sentence writes itself after three years of use.)

I realize there is a temptation to accept these invitations if only to prove (to whom? yourself?) that, even though retired, you aren't on the shelf or out to pasture some place. But having your name on a program or a letter-head doesn't fool anybody—assuming anybody's even looking. And so, while it's good, even essential, to stay active, it's not good to become fake-active at things you don't really enjoy.

Finally, retirement raises, with a vengeance and a huge yawn, the subject of boredom. Since boredom looms so large throughout our lives, but especially in middle age and beyond, I'd thought of devoting a separate chapter to it. But since it also strikes many of us with suffocating intensity after retirement, I decided it belongs in this one, but rather as a kind of postscript or coda. So let me just say at this point that boredom is a crime against oneself, and if you haven't learned that by the time you're fifty you haven't learned much worth knowing.

Successful retirement requires preparation. And the test of success is often said to be when you wonder aloud how you ever found the time to hold a 9:00 A.M.–6:00 P.M. job; in other words, the busier you are, the better. But the question arises, busy at what? Bingo?

So preparation means, first, sorting out the things you enjoy doing, like bird watching, from those you don't, like fund raising, and then making plans that will enable you to devote much more time to ornithology than to philanthropy after retirement. Just make sure the plans include something active and demanding (it wouldn't be bird watching in my case), or you will find yourself, like so many demobilized wage earners, withering away on putting greens and park benches with no vital functions to perform.

Preparation also means brushing up certain hard-earned credentials that can make retirement more pleasurable. For example, when I left *Newsday,* I kept abreast of what was happening in the newspaper business because I felt like teaching journalism in a structured setting—something I'd never tried. So I tried it, and it was work I enjoyed while it lasted but not, I knew, as a profession to embark upon at age sixty. Teaching journalism, like teaching many academic courses, is the province of the tenured faculty with their advanced degrees. They don't necessarily teach the subject any better than those of us who have earned our living in the trade, but it seems unfair, somehow, to trespass on their turf.

Being recognized as an authority of sorts on a few subjects (Africa, Russia, and newspapering are among mine) is a useful asset in retirement if you like to attend occasional conferences, write articles, or deliver speeches. Some of these can be fun if you space them far enough apart, and they help forestall that easy slide into a passive retirement routine.

In preparing to retire, it's also advisable to overload the circuits at first—to take on more commitments than you really intend to continue. Some things that sound boring might not be, and vice versa. When you find out, shuck off what doesn't turn you on. In my case, I resigned in 1981 alone as chairman of *Geo* magazine's editorial advisory board, as a trustee of the Kress Foundation, as a director of the Alan Guttmacher Institute, as a governor of the Block Island Club—as well as an available unpaid speaker to all but a handful of local clubs and civic associations. I have a few more affiliations picked for termination in 1982. This allows me more time for things that give me satisfaction—like writing, or getting involved in political and other activities that may increase my children's and grandchildren's chances of living in a saner, safer and habitable world. That's the least we can do, we who have been around for a while and appreciate how dangerous the world has become.

In short, prepare your retirement with the attitude that

you aren't so much retiring from a job as you are embarking on a variety of activities you've always wanted to indulge in but never seemed to have the time or opportunity for. And it usually happens to be the truth.

On an island where Sim and I now own a gift shop and art gallery, we rent space to an ice cream parlor that was built by and belongs to a middle-aged friend who quit his job as a public relations executive with a hotel chain to become a full-time carpenter, handyman, truck gardener and now local ice cream magnate. Bob's retirement was in no sense a slackening off but rather a redirection of his energies.

Another example: thirty years ago, vacationing in Sicily, Sim and I met another Bob, a Cleveland industrialist who'd made a comfortable fortune and then retired, in his fifties. Walking together along the beach at Taormina, I could see he was restless, and I wasn't surprised to get a letter from him soon after saying that he and his wife had settled down in Rome where he had become administrator of a division of the Marshall Plan for Italy. After three years, his batteries recharged by a new challenge, he went back to Cleveland, started another business, made a second fortune—and died last year in his mid-eighties.

Both these men had probably escaped what the *Wall Street Journal* has called "executive burnout." This is a condition apparently affecting a growing number of unhappy corporate managers who experience "feelings of frustration, cynicism and helplessness." The paper attributed the increase in burnout cases to the fact that "people now expect more from their jobs than just a paycheck."

So I suspect early retirement—or more precisely, late midlife changes of occupation—will become more common in the years ahead; and as one who's tried it, I recommend it. There'll be holdouts, of course. "It's become socially acceptable, even chic, to say you're burnt-out," one management consultant told the *Journal*. So I guess the chic folks will stay miserable while those of us seated below the salt sample other lifestyles.

One last observation about preparing for retirement. It's easier for people in so-called creative occupations to clean out their desks and walk out than it is for those who do work that can't be performed at home. Writers, artists, and craftsmen of all kinds are lucky: not only can they often do as well (except for company benefits) on their own, but they adapt better to the solitude of the self-employed. In his latest book, Graham Greene has gone so far as to liken the creative life to survival: "Writing is a form of therapy. Sometimes I wonder how all those who do not write, compose or paint can manage to escape the madness, the melancholia, the panic fear which is inherent in the human situation."

But there are executives whose only skills are administrative. Retirees from these noncreative jobs (like managers whose impact on the finished product is at best indirect, and assembly line workers whose real life is often away from the workplace) have a harder time. Some retired executives, like my father, occupy many of their final years meticulously sorting and classifying the mounds of correspondence, documents and snapshots accumulated during a lifetime and never to be looked at again. Other executives, deprived by retirement of the corporate courtiers and perquisites of office, turn to sports, to drink, to psychiatrists, or to long-neglected hobbies. Blue-collar workers usually have active hobbies to which they've fled for years from the monotony of their jobs. These can either be essentially juvenile pastimes, like beer-fueled hunting and bowling outings, or gainful alternative occupations like, say, cabinetmaking. But all who reach middle age should know that whatever they choose to do at this period in time will affect both the tranquillity and vitality of all their remaining years—which could be more numerous than they might reasonably expect. (How could my mother possibly have anticipated that, at ninety-three, she would be visiting her ninety-five-year-old brother-in-law in a nursing home every few days?)

So let's face it: retirement can be quite a wrench, psychologically, for anyone to whom work has been the justification and the centerpiece of his or her life. But assuming thoughtful preparation, it's a condition that has many more pluses than minuses:

- You work almost as much but waste far less time going to and from your place of business; and you also waste less time on the job because you are fully in charge of your time and how you spend it.
- You have the pleasure of *not* doing certain things, like attending company picnics or getting up at 7 A.M. whether you feel like getting up or not.
- You shed social obligations right and left and restrict your circle of friends to a congenial hard core of intimates.
- You find time to help others—not just by donating to the Salvation Army—but by teaching, writing, counseling young people, doing things for your community you never had the time for when the salaried job was all-consuming.
- You find you have more time to indulge in sports that give you pleasure. Just take care not to get too good at any of them, which is unlikely at this age, or they can dominate and thus diminish your life. I've seen

jovial foursomes coming off the eighteenth green—
none with a handicap of less than 24; but I've yet
to see any happy-looking low handicap players at the
end of a round: everyone has at least one double-
bogey or four-putt to brood about.
You can at long last try new things—things done for
the first time. Try soaring. Visit Cuba. Learn to sketch.
Just doing something new will make you feel younger.
And when you feel younger, it shows. Remember my
stab at defining the outer limits of middle age some
chapters ago: it happens when you begin to perceive
yourself in decline—and others, sensing it, begin regarding you as old.

Retirement, then, can and should be like changing jobs
at any age—a rejuvenating experience and the start of a
new chapter in your life, however near you may actually be
to the end of the book.

The minuses of retirement are more precisely risks to
guard against. For example, it can be tempting to do
nothing at all, especially if your retirement is from a dull
job and comes with a comfortable pension. For people
accustomed to lives of routine tasks and routine distrac-
tions, idleness can seem like a decided improvement, and
a completed crossword puzzle a proud achievement.

Also, people with lifetime hobbies are often disap-
pointed in retirement because, while it might have been fun
to escape to the basement after a dull day at the office and
a tempestuous meal with the loved ones in order to carve
ship models, spending all day in the basement can be
too much.

And there are restless dreams, for a year or so after
retirement, in which you find yourself rejected and ignored by old associates. These dreams pass. And what

should also pass is any resentment initially felt by husbands when they discover or are told in an outburst of candor by their still-working wives that their pensions are less than their mates' earnings. So what? Marriage should be a joint enterprise with no perpetually dominant breadwinner. Tell that to the marines.

To make these critical retirement years, that could easily comprise a third of your life, as pleasurable and rewarding as possible, let me offer some suggestions based on my so far limited but contemplative experience.

Do something every year you've never done before. I've said it already but it's worth repeating. Since 1979, when I retired from routine, Sim, Jan, Suzy and I toured the Baltic republics of the Soviet Union—a part of the world I'd always wanted to see, and Suzy and I crossed the Arctic Circle, into Finland's reindeer country; I taught seminars; I took a long-deferred trip on a canal barge with Sim and. Suzy through southern France; I sold pieces to four magazines I'd never written for before; I learned hypnotism; I attended a two-week Aspen Institute executive seminar as a presidential fellow, and enjoyed it much more than I expected.

Next year, Sim and I plan to go to Zimbabwe, where we have old friends, and I'll also spend time teaching at universities in Virginia and Ohio. I've always wanted to translate a French novel—I may do that too. And write another children's book. And I have other ideas, knowing that the more I plan to do the more I have to look forward to.

Politics are okay in retirement if you have the energy and the body chemistry to stand the pace. If not, be careful of people who approach you with the two phrases that have lured many an innocent citizen into a bruising, expensive campaign: one, you have a lot of friends in the state; two, there's no one else who could do the job.

Beware of drifting into a daily routine of simulated activity—such as waiting for the mail to be delivered and then dutifully reading all the commercial junk that arrives. There's usually enough so that you can spend the rest of the day filling out the fake questionnaires, entering the phony contests, and answering a heap of correspondence from strangers seeking favors—and then kid yourself into believing you've accomplished something. It's a deceptively easy routine to slip into for former executives conditioned to regard the processing of pieces of paper as real work.

If you are truly lazy or just lack energy, you're better off finding a real if undemanding part-time job with a respectable title—president of the historical society, official town archivist, chairman of some permanent worthwhile bipartisan committee.

If you like dogs, get a young dog now, even though it may outlive you. It will take you outdoors on cold days and persuade you to throw sticks and other things for it to retrieve. It will do you good and might even liven up your old dog who now bestirs himself only at mealtimes.

Think hard before moving to the sunbelt. Constant warm weather is debilitating and conducive to torpor, a condition in which you aren't even aware of loafing. The climate is also dehydrating, which encourages drinking beverages that can aggravate the torpor. It's no accident that for centuries the southern parts of most western industrialized countries (and China, India, and Japan as well) were the poorest and most backward. (In the southern hemisphere, of course, the situation is reversed: tropical *northern* Brazil is the depressed part of the nation.)

Climate aside, it's best to be where you feel you have

roots under foot. Mine are in Connecticut. Our town is populated with my cousins and the cemetery full of family names. At the two hundred fiftieth anniversary celebration of Canaan parish last year, my mother sat in the front row. I know where home is. In retirement, it's a good place to be close to.

Don't worry about what other people think about your decision to drop out of the marathon before the finish line. Don't try to tell them how active you are on the sidelines. For they don't care (unless they scent gossip); people, as I've said earlier, care only about those relatively few people they love and about those who might give them some assistance or pleasure.

Finally, don't feel you've become a quitter. You have simply chosen to work at something more satisfying and more creative: at living.

Now we come at last to the greatest threat, other than disabling illness, to the enjoyment of your retirement years: the stifling, soggy blanket of boredom.

Earlier I called boredom a crime against oneself; for isn't there something felonious in deliberately choosing to spoil any part of the limited time we are allotted on earth? Getting drunk and taking dope are also self-inflicted crimes but at least they offer some momentary pleasure; boredom doesn't even do that.

Fortunately, by the time you're ready to retire, you should have learned how to minimize or even eliminate a good many boring episodes in your life.

You have learned, presumably, that much of what we call conversation is boring. It consists of reciting anecdotes dealing mostly with minor woes and mishaps (high prices, physical ailments, mechanical difficulties) that are of little or no interest to the other party or parties to the conversation. They listen, however, with feigned attention, waiting for the opening that will allow them to relate *their* anecdotes. Very little of the information thus exchanged makes a point (except that things break and people are not to be trusted) or even reaches a conclusion; the anecdotes normally just drift to a halt as if the narrator ran out of breath. Some are told mainly to enhance the ego of the teller: realtors will discuss mortgages partly, if unwittingly, to exhibit their expertise; so do others with a subject they know well and which they therefore feel secure in discussing.

But at a certain time of life, you don't really have to sit and listen anymore. You can get up, excuse yourself, go to the john and not come back.

You also learn to avoid people who drop names and places. They do tell anecdotes with a point, but the point is obvious: "I happened to be sitting next to Elizabeth Taylor on a flight to Istanbul last week and she told me. . . ."

Be careful of people who talk or write pompously or solemnly. During the 1942 brownout in New York, signs were put up by the civil defense authorities in apartment house entrances that read: "Illumination is required to be extinguished prior to vacating the premises." Whoever translated "Turn out the lights when you leave" into that jargon would not be my choice for a dinner companion.

On the other hand, E. B. White once said he knew he'd married the right wife when he first heard her refer to dental floss as tooth twine. How we speak and how we write are good clues to who we are.

That's why, to avoid boring entrapments, be wary of people who say things like, "As I always say. . . ." "Let me tell ya something. . . ." or "To make a long story short. . . ." Be wary, too, of those who converse in cliches or who complain a lot or who talk too much—as if they could no longer receive, only transmit.

Most television is boring—and I've never been what they used to call an egghead. On most shows the laughter is nervous, the situations unreal, the adults childish, and the outcome predictable. I still miss "The Honeymooners." A long spell of television watching, in hospital for instance, leaves me feeling hollow. I think I'd rather spend an entire afternoon repairing a television set (if I knew how) than watching one.

Most large parties are boring. Luckily, the bigger they are, the easier it is to leave early. Best is not to go; next best is not to stay.

All banquets and most testimonial dinners are boring. A few years back, I had to attend one given by some Long Island chamber of commerce because I was the speaker. When I walked in I was surprised to see that all the guests were black. After a drink and some small talk with the notables, it dawned on us that I was at the wrong function; mine was one flight up in the catering complex. It would have made little difference: the affairs were interchangeable, certainly as to food and possibly as to speeches.

Meetings, especially numbering more than five people, are usually so boring you think your watch has stopped.

All but a few speeches are boring. Mine are among the few that aren't because I've devised a crowd-pleasing formula over the years: announce a fifteen-minute time limit— this immediately relaxes the audience and captures its attention. Tell one good joke. State a fact. Give an illustration of the fact. Tell another good joke. Sit down, on time. You'll be asked again.

Group travel is boring, yet it's a favorite pastime of the middle-aged and the retired. To be enjoyable, I think travel needs a purpose other than photographing monuments to justify the fatigue and discomfort it entails in the jet age. I've normally traveled in pursuit of a story or on government orders. But in 1977, I tried a Nile river cruise with family and friends. It might have been fun if we'd been antiquarians, archeologists, or pharaoh freaks— for that's what travel directors in Egypt must assume all tourists are.

There's only one thing more boring—having to look at the color slides when the travelers come home.

Of course if you want to find out how really boring a holiday can be, you can always visit a state-run facility in a communist country. After seeing the official resort in Sinaia, Rumania, I could understand why boredom, more than repression, is the ultimate Achilles' heel of the Soviet system.

I could go on, but you know what I'm saying. Retirement can be imperiled by boredom but not if you take precautions. Unblock your curiosity about how things work, and how to fix them when they don't. Pause before you shut out *all* new people from your circle of friends; some may become your last best friends. And hardly anyone is *totally* uninteresting. (If you find some who are, that in itself makes them interesting.) Have some projects on your agenda—more than you can handle. Take courses that can help you master new skills; it's never too late. Learn to play a musical instrument—it doesn't have to be a piano. Seek out new experiences. Plan ahead.

And retirement needn't take place at sixty-five; if you make plans and your employer is cooperative, it can be sooner or, if you wish, later. Timing is always important but seldom more so than in these windup years.

When you do retire, don't, above all, let others make you feel old. The young may be more nimble but the elderly are likely to be smarter. If younger people think of you as over the hill—so what? You've done things they can't imagine and seen things they can't even visualize. Of course, you're more likely to die sooner, but is that anything to be ashamed of? I think our society induces people to think so.

In my town, they sell reduced fare railroad tickets to senior citizens. You just have to produce proof that you're more than sixty-five. But I actually know of four or five men who would rather pay full fare than have the conductor know they are senior citizens.

Accept and proclaim your age, whatever it is, and you can be middle-aged for as long as you feel like it.

13

DEATH

AT SEVENTEEN, my daughter Suzy agreed with me that her most ingrained traits were stubbornness, sensitivity, shyness and a kind of aggressive honesty. When she was five, stubbornness predominated.

"Suzy," I told her one morning, "eat your cereal. You *have* to eat your cereal."

"No, I don't," she retorted with the feisty impudence of the very young. "I don't *have* to do anything. Except die."

What made her reply so precocious is that she was stating a truth that is accepted by everyone but not always *felt* by anyone until something happens to him or to her, normally during this period called middle age. Even brushes with death earlier in life leave no lasting traces:

I came very close to dying from scarlet fever as a child, saw bullets strike a few feet away in wartime, missed a fatal flight on a BOAC Comet by an hour, swerved (instinctively) out of a right-hand lane on a Scottish highway seconds before a truck came thundering around a blind curve. Dangers abound, and it's a wonder so many of us survive into old age, let alone adulthood, in a civilization so cluttered with lethal machinery. But none of my near misses left me with the sense that I'd actually caught a glimpse of the grim reaper until my heart attack, when I felt his attendant presence out in the vestibule of the intensive care unit. And that glimpse, or encounter (like the death of a spouse or close friend) does change your outlook on mortality; never again do you consider death as something that happens only to other people.

Yet death strikes repeatedly and at random all through the years preceding middle age. In the summer of 1963, I found myself sitting at a table in Joe Alsop's garden in Washington with Jack Kennedy, who was then president; Lady Ormsby-Gore, the wife of the British ambassador; and Mary Pinchot Meyer, an artist Kennedy and I had both known since our schooldays and with whom I'd been hopelessly in love during my teen years. Had an old gypsy fortune teller come up at that moment and predicted that three of us would die violently within eighteen months, I doubt if we'd have paid her much attention. Yet Kennedy was assassinated that fall, Mary was murdered while strolling along the Potomac in 1964, and Lady Ormsby-Gore later died in a car crash in Ireland.

You can react to the certainty of your own death in at least three ways: immaturely, with depression and even panic; obsessively, like Gore Vidal who admitted in a recent interview that, at fifty-five, he thinks about death all the time (I wonder what there is to think about); or calmly, accepting the inevitable as something that needn't be feared if only because so many people are doing it all the time. How we die, not the act of dying, is the only thing worth being concerned about. A long, losing battle with cancer, an immobilizing stroke, the creeping degeneration of Parkinson's disease—these are to be dreaded. We can only hope to be as fortunate as Adlai Stevenson who, at sixty-five, on a mission to London, strolling in summer twilight to a dinner party in the company of a beautiful woman, felt suddenly dizzy and fell to the pavement, where, moments later, a doctor pronounced him dead.

Fear of death is really fear of the unknown—of Hamlet's "undiscovered country." Our world, for all of its miseries, is our home, the only home we've known, and leaving it for the first and probably last time can't help but make anyone apprehensive. A few people, like O. Henry, have been able to think of their ultimate destination as the place they originally came from. "Turn up the lights," he demanded on his deathbed. "I don't want to go home in the dark."

Once you have confronted and accepted the inevitability (and perhaps imminence) of your own mortality, then it dawns on you that there's no reason to think of it as a fearsome prospect. This revelation usually takes place in middle age, when every day's obit page contains one or more familiar names, thus assuring us we'll have plenty of congenial company over there—if such a place exists.

Whenever I think about dying, which is not very often now that I'm able to face it with a certain equanimity, I imagine that we are all in canoes drifting rapidly downstream in the canyon of a fast-moving river, drawn by an inexorable current to the great falls rumbling in the distance. Some of us try to paddle vainly against the current, or to cling to the sheer walls of the gorge, and some capsize into suicide and drown prematurely; but the rest of us know there is no escaping the final plunge over the edge and down the foaming wall of white water.

The river is crowded with people and canoes; it's our last and greatest adventure, and there is no longer anything to be afraid of.

There's no set formula for getting over one's fear of death; everybody has to work through it alone. I'll take my cue from Shakespeare, from *The Tempest,* where Prospero says, "We are such stuff as dreams are made on, and our little life is rounded with a sleep." For death may well be eternal sleep. The only alternative I can even conceive of would be an unlikely afterlife consisting of more of the same in some kind of reincarnation a few centuries hence. I'd prefer the big sleep.

The traditional Christian alternatives, a beatific heaven or a demonic hell—forever—are just too farfetched even to contemplate.

Nor is the act of dying unpleasant, according to those who have suffered temporary cardiac arrest and been revived; they say that at the end there is neither pain nor fear—only a feeling of peaceful release. Six of these "returnees" were interviewed recently on Phil Donahue's show, and none had experienced that fear of the unknown from which organized religion derives so much of its power.

It's often, and I think, wrongly, assumed that people become more religious as they get older. Atheists say that God is simply an invention of those who can't bear to face death's awful mysteries alone. And during World War II, it was popular to say that "there are no atheists in fox-holes," implying that when soldiers turned to the Lord they did so only out of fear. Personally, I haven't noticed any religious upsurge among the middle-aged; in fact,

the most ardent believers I've encountered, like my son
Peter, are mostly under thirty-five, many of them dis-
illusioned and now born-again alumni and alumnae of
the counterculture of the sixties. Growing older and
presumably coming closer to Judgment Day hasn't made
many converts out of my contemporaries. Many of them,
in fact, begin to question the spiritual pieties they memo-
rized in childhood and start reading irreverent satires like
Mark Twain's small masterpiece, *Letters from the Earth*.
My wife Sim, raised as a Roman Catholic, eight years in
a convent school, is less and less inclined to enter a church
with each passing year.

My own religious beliefs are rather spare but sufficient
for my needs. At least they don't clash with whatever
common sense I've acquired from the experience of living
sixty-odd years. No, I am not an atheist: I would no more
presume to deny the existence of God than to affirm it. I
go along with Kurt Vonnegut, who has described himself
as "a skeptic about the divinity of Christ and a scorner
of the notion that there is a God who cares how we are
or what we do." This makes it hard for me to go to church
(except as a quiet place to meditate when there is no
service going on) without feeling like a hypocrite amid a
congregation reciting credos with which I can't agree.

And yet we all need to believe in something . . . tran-
scendental; or at the very least in something that gives us
reason to believe there is some point to living according
to a set of principles or a philosophy incorporating the
golden rule. Some people need the fear of hell or the hope
of heaven or the voice of ecclesiastical authority to beef up
their consciences; others, like me, figure that doing right
is simply more satisfying than doing wrong and that our
consciences may indeed provide the only conclusive evidence of God's existence. And if such a divine entity exists

(I have a hard time saying He as I can't imagine God as having a gender) then we should perhaps surprise It by doing our level best to make the human experiment on planet earth succeed. So I suppose I am sustained by a certain *esprit de corps* for the family of man, imperfect as we have always been. And again like Vonnegut, I would want to be able to say to God on Judgment Day, "I was a very good person even though I did not believe in you."

I started this chapter talking about death; it's natural I should now be discussing religion, since death is when we supposedly meet our maker. And besides, we tend, in middle age, to question and rethink all sorts of assumptions that we've carried around with us, like toys that don't work, ever since childhood.

Religion, for example, never played a big part in my life. I remember attending church with my parents from time to time, usually at Easter and at funerals, ambling reluctantly to Sunday school, passing the plate after the obligatory service, squirming with boredom in the choir loft of a boarding school chapel—and never thinking about God except when I had to as part of a college philosophy course.

Then, about eleven years ago, my son called us from Illinois, where he was hitchhiking to California to work for Cesar Chavez, and informed us he'd become a Christian. He'd been a lot of things, from a numismatician to a political activist, so we took the news in stride. But he's been a Christian ever since, and has taught me that to be honestly a Christian you have to accept it all and believe it all—the fables, the miracles, the personal jealous God, the authority of the Bible. There's no such thing as quasi-Christianity: Christ is our saviour and he died for our sins and he rose from the dead—or he isn't, and didn't. I feel no kinship with all-out Christians but I can respect them as I never could those who call themselves Christians but choose to be selective about what they believe. And I feel the same about quasi Moslems or quasi Hindus or whatever the name of the lodge.

Peter and I get along quite well, but the totality of his faith has limited our relationship in that our conversations end by tacit and mutual consent at the water's edge of religion. He has given up trying to convert me, and I have no intention of challenging his beliefs; these in any event are beyond the reach of rational argument. I suspect that, like all highly intelligent believers, his own reason is occasionally in conflict with his faith, which is why Bible study is a never-ending activity among many Christians. They must keep going back to the source for reassurance, especially when the acts of their God must appear so often capricious if not downright cruel. Fanaticism can result; for as the Canadian writer Robertson Davies has aptly defined it, fanaticism is "over-compensation for doubt."

Now and then Peter and I brush up against the subject. Not long ago, he observed that the Pentagon "worshipped" weapons. I thought the verb was a little strong until he explained that people worship what they rely on: it can be money, or power, or themselves. That was how he defined God—what you can rely on. And when we spoke of the hereafter, he rejected the possibility of the big sleep. Hell exists for Peter. It is, he said, a place where God is absent and evil is rampant, and it is reserved for all who reject Him during their life on earth.

I listen to Peter, but without alarm. He has found his own kind of peace, as personal as is mine. And, as positive as he sounds about a stern deity, I cannot believe that God is anything but benevolent; in which case, what is there to fear?

Of course, the laid-back arrogance of the overtly devout can be irritating. But if you are not one of them, remember how desperate is their need to believe, to *know* that they are loved, looked after and cared for by a solicitous Lord. Some came to Christ stumbling out of the drug scene; others had suffered emotional breakdowns; many, I'm convinced, would resort to suicide if something were suddenly to shatter the foundations of their faith.

Not all, but most of the intensely religious younger people I've met remind me of patients in wheelchairs, content to have the Lord guide and propel them in the right direction and no longer even interested in trying to walk unaided. Their Bibles are never out of reach; they cling to them as a drowning man clutches a life preserver. I feel like an alien among them. One Thanksgiving, Peter persuaded me to attend services at an Episcopalian church that had turned "charismatic" and quintupled its membership. The atmosphere was buoyant and rather unstructured: there was lots of singing and people held hands and now and then broke out in spontaneous prayers and hallelujahs. I found it both soothing and cheery—everything my own church experience had not been—but I still felt I was among strangers. Were all these people genuinely this happy—or only straining hard to be?

At the end of the service, the pastor was at the door and said he hoped he'd see me again, but I've never gone back nor has Peter asked me. I've reached a stage in life where I'm no longer a likely prospect for recruitment; I'm on good terms with myelf and, I believe, with whatever higher authority may exist.

And I rather like the mystery of our being here and then dying and perhaps finding out . . . something. I think many others who have reached middle age and beyond feel as I do, and for this reason do not embrace the certainty and security of man-made religion as they might be expected to with death coming closer. Mystery is more fun.

"As you grow older," said the author Henry Miller, at eighty, "you only realize how many secrets there must be. Your sense of wonder increases. The more one penetrates the realm of knowledge, the more puzzling everything becomes. I find life more and more mysterious."

In fact, life is both more and less mysterious than it was during the centuries when the Bible was being written. Science has opened up whole new vistas of exploration, often in the teeth of the religious establishment, and these have raised new questions about mankind's origins. But science has also answered questions once considered beyond human comprehension.

"Indeed," wrote the sociobiologist Edward O. Wilson in *On Human Nature,*

The origin of the universe in the big bang of fifteen billion years ago, as deduced by astronomers and physicists, is far more awesome that the first chapter of Genesis or the Ninevite epic of Gilgamesh. When the scientists project physical processes backward to that moment with the aid of mathematical models they are talking about everything—literally everything—and when they move forward in time to pulsars, supernovas, and the collision of black holes they probe distances and mysteries beyond the imaginings of earlier generations. Recall how God lashed Job with concepts meant to overwhelm the human mind:

Who is this whose ignorant words
cloud my design in darkness?
Brace yourself and stand up like a man;
I will ask questions and you shall answer

. . . .

Have you descended to the springs of the sea
or walked in the unfathomable deep?
Have the gates of death been revealed to you?
Have you ever seen the door-keepers of the place of
darkness?
Have you comprehended the vast expanse of the world?
Come, tell me all this, if you know.

And yes, we do know and we have told. Jehovah's
challenges have been met and scientists have pressed
on to uncover and to solve even greater puzzles. The
physical basis of life is known; we understand ap-
proximately how and when it started on earth. New
species have been created in the laboratory and evolu-
tion has been traced at the molecular level. Genes
can be spliced from one kind of organism into
another. Molecular biologists have most of the knowledge needed to create elementary forms of life. Our
machines, settled on Mars, have transmitted pan-
oramic views and the results of chemical soil analysis.
Could the Old Testament writers have conceived of
such activity? And still the process of great scientific
discovery gathers momentum.

Wilson is talking about the scarcely tapped human
potential for exploring the unknown, for seeking answers
to the eternal riddles of who we are and why we are here.
The poet Archibald MacLeish has linked the driving
curiosity of scientific humanism to the Jeffersonian revolution which he says "has never been achieved," and sees
it as the great unfinished business of future generations:

The promise of the revolution of man, is that he
can and will prove himself capable of governing himself, capable of changing and enlarging life, capable of

realizing on this earth the kind of life that nobody (although everybody talks about it) has ever really lived. The Jeffersonian shift was a shift away from that subservient, obedient attitude toward life and the rules of God, the belief that God is the mover and man is the sheep whom the Shepherd will take care of. Today even the most fundamental fundamentalist would be shocked if he were told to sit and fold his hands and wait for God to solve all our tremendous problems. Reading Jefferson's words, you can almost feel in the seat of your pants the enormous heist that you have been given. Maybe you've been kicked over the wall into eternal disaster, but I don't think so.

Those unable to feel the heist understandably turn to the comforting rituals of religion. For it's as necessary to believe in something as it is to live as though life were both important and everlasting. The alternative—believing in nothing, discerning no purpose to our lives—leads to the nausea that Jean-Paul Sartre once described in a novel with that title.

All right, we've digressed, and what I've outlined is faith enough for me—and perhaps also for all curious, perplexed but temperamentally unworshipful middle-aged people faced with the solo assignment of coming to terms with their own mortality; or, as Robert Penn Warren has put it, the terms you make with life in relation to death: "You don't wait for death; you live for death."

And of course the devout resent us secular, or scientific humanists more than they do the misguided heathen who can always be considered potential candidates for redemption. (The missionary calling is a tough one, though, no question about that; in Guinea I met a Protestant divine who'd lived thirty-seven years far out in the bush and whose single African convert had recently backslid to Islam. Otherwise, the missionary had managed only to translate the Bible into fula, a spoken dialect that no one reads.)

Having, as I said, caught a glimpse of Mr. Thanatos, I've lost my fear of him. He is no grim, skeletal figure with a scythe, come to lead me to Charon's barge. I think of Mr. T. more as a bureaucratic timekeeper making his appointed rounds. As you get older, you may catch sight of him from time to time, because he's more likely to be in your demographic neighborhood. Sometimes he goes away, and sometimes not.

Death's measured approach makes you want to communicate, to talk more about things that are neither frivolous nor solemn with friends and with strangers, too. This is certainly one reason for my writing this book. If you are a sceptic about an afterlife and, like most people, hanker after a few crumbs of immortality, you want to make something that will outlast you and that will be read or seen or heard and somehow appreciated by somebody living in posterity. None of the hundreds of thousands of words I've written in my lifetime are likely to be looked at again, except perhaps for one children's book, another that might be of use to some scholars, and possibly this one, assuming middle age remains a permanent feature of the human condition. But this is plenty. If you remember World War II, it's like writing "Kilroy was here" on a wall in a faraway town and then moving on.

There's certainly no other good reason for sitting in front of a typewriter a couple of hours of each day for nearly a year. I've no idea how much time I have left (not a hell of a lot considering my medical record) , so whatever motivates me is clearly not the possibility of best-sellerdom or a career in literature. It's rather this urge to communicate with others, in a sometimes intensely personal way, which strikes some of us in the middle and waning years of our lives.

This urge is as characteristic of these years as is our intolerance of triviality (unless we are trivial people ourselves) and also our protective shield of stoicism. I don't mean stoic in its religious sense but as shorthand for that attitude that enables us to anesthetize ourselves to strong feelings (no feeling is bad but pain can be worse) and to smooth down the emotional hills and valleys that make the landscape of youth appear so manic and strenuous from afar. The advantages of this kind of stoicism are that good moments (a spontaneous gesture of affection) are doubly welcome because unexpected; and bad moments (a spouse's verbal dart) are less hurtful because the Novocaine is working.

I am reading a torn clipping (I have a bonfire-sized collection of clippings) that quotes a psychiatrist named Dr. Horton who says, "One of the most persistent human needs is that for solace. Solace is a resource that soothes pain and great psychic stress, it gives us a neutral framework so we can cope with changing circumstances. Human suffering is ubiquitous, and we need to find tangible or intangible relief for it, as long as we live."

I'll buy that, too, especially the last phrase. Coping with life's vicissitudes is something we do right up to the end.

And at the end, I want only to be able to look ahead, into the unknown, without apprehension, and to look back at the things I remember best in my life with much more nostalgia than remorse.

14

MEMORIES

HAPPINESS, according to a frequently quoted remark attributed to Dr. Albert Schweitzer, is good health and a bad memory. No one who's been sick will quarrel about the health part but a bad memory is desirable only if most of the things you are able to remember are unpleasant or depressing.

Good memories can soothe and brighten our middle and late years, just as bad ones can sour them. That's why it's important, and never too late, to keep adding to our store of pleasant recollections. For life in middle age and beyond does tend to become increasingly retrospective. "Don't look back," we are told, "there's nothing you can do about the past anyway." True enough. But unless you're subject to convenient spells of amnesia, this is far easier said than done. Night dreams, day dreams, familiar sights, sounds and smells, as well as incidents that summon up images from the recesses of our minds, simply cannot be suppressed or denied. Moreover, in middle age, you can't help but think more about the past if only because there is more of it piling up every day; and even if you can't change or wipe out the things that have happened to you, you can certainly learn from them. Memory has its uses, not the least of which is the substance and continuity it gives to our lives. I liked what George Will, the columnist, recently had to say about this:

"It is said that God gave us memory so we could have roses in winter," he wrote. "But it is also true that without memory we would not have a self in any season. The more memories you have, the more 'you' you have. That is why, as Swift said, 'no wise man ever wished to be younger.' "

Never has Swift's comment been as appropriate as today, in our time, the time of those of us who are older than forty-five. If you are in this demographic group, consider yourself lucky, for you caught at least a glimpse and can cherish some memories of a more relaxed and exuberant world—a world that vanished, probably forever, in the space of a few years under the impact of television, jet planes, nuclear fission, computer technology and the population explosion.

My generation, the one now middle-aged and older, grew up in a relatively optimistic, manageable, and safe environment. Even during the great depression, the unemployed men selling apples for a nickel on New York street corners seemed to us docile, more humiliated than angry, and hopeful that things would soon get better. Popular fads were not as supercharged and the national attention span was less fickle. Take the 1970s. I can't think of anything that decade will be remembered for except possibly jogging, oil, cocaine, Watergate, computer games, discos and CB radios. And all will have been forgotten or replaced by the end of the eighties, if they haven't been already. (How long has it been since you warned a good buddy about a bear in a plain wrapper?)

In our time, plumbers and electricians and carpenters came when summoned, and doctors made house calls; hardly anyone had ever met, let alone consulted, a psychiatrist, and nobody knew anybody who used drugs, though it was whispered around that Gene Krupa, Benny Goodman's drummer, smoked reefers. Our music, swing music, made us want to dance, to hold each other close, even to cry when we heard some special, evocative song two summers later—like Martha Tilton belting out "It's Been So Long." For us city kids, the parks were safe, at first for gang warfare with cap pistols, later for touch football, even later, after dark, for necking—then the ultimate in adolescent sexual expectations.

Radio was the obligato to my homework: the Texaco Fire Chief, Stoopnagle and Budd, Kate Smith. Radio stretched our imaginations: all we heard were the voices; the rest had to be filled in. (Most of us thought that Amos and Andy were black—or, as we would have said, Negro.) Our magazines were *Boy's Life*, which I sold door to door, *Liberty*, and *Ballyhoo*. Skin books like *Playboy* and *Penthouse* were inconceivable.

We never thought about pollution; the air looked clean and smelled pretty good, and smog was unheard of. On camping trips, we never hesitated to drink from the streams and ponds. Summer and winter the woods were quiet: motorcycles were seldom seen and snowmobiles not yet invented.

All this and much more is stored away in my memory,

and if I took just one sip of Ovaltine (or cod liver oil or a chocolate malted), or brushed my teeth with Ipana or smelled a cake of Lifebuoy soap, a torrent of detail would rush into my consciousness, the way it did for Marcel Proust as he dipped his *madeleine* in a cup of tea while writing *Remembrance of Things Past.*

And it would be good stuff, mostly, fun to dwell on and chuckle over. Like Lifebuoy. Nobody could stand the soap; it smelled like disinfectant. But we all dreaded "B.O.," a condition the soap was guaranteed to cure, according to the certificate, suitable for framing, that I received in exchange for ten cents and which designated me as a Lifebuoy Health Guard. (At fourteen, I also became a member of the Aqua Velva After Shave Club, which prompted my father to suggest that one of my uncles, the one with the flushed face, apply to join the Four Roses Society.)

Any travel was an adventure in the days of my generation's youth. Faraway places were exotic, sure to be different—rickshaws in Hong Kong, camels in Cairo, wild men in Borneo, and no Hiltons, Hyatts or MacDonalds anywhere. As for Africa, it belonged to Tarzan and his companions, not today's air-conditioned tourist buses.

We took trains when I was a kid—usually, for me, an overnight train to Mansfield, Ohio, the headquarters of the Ohio Brass Company, for which my father sold insulators. What do I remember best? The hissing of the steam in Penn station, the heavy cutlery and linen tablecloths in the diner, waking at night in my berth behind the thick green curtains and looking out at some deserted depot, wondering where we might be; the commotion in the men's washroom in the morning, the smell of shaving soap and tobacco smoke, the hard leather seats, the brass spitoons; the anticipation of breakfast: buckwheat cakes, thick slabs of bacon, warm blueberry muffins, cocoa; the excitement of being in—Ohio.

Ocean liners were even more fun, not only for kids, and they remained the only way to cross the Atlantic until the late thirties. We went over every other summer because my father had Europe as part of his territory, and the company paid our fare; mother and I stayed with relatives in Normandy while he sold insulators all the way from Finland to Italy.

There was nothing like being a kid of nine or eleven and going up that gangplank in the evening knowing you had six days of freedom, mischief, exploration and adventure ahead. Soon the great whistle would blast its farewell to New York and the ship would start vibrating. And in the morning, you'd wake up in a berth that was pitching and rolling and quickly scramble down to see who there might be of your age aboard to join forces with. Really rough days were the best—walking was hazardous, most adults were seasick, and the spray lashed the open decks. At eleven in the morning they served chicken broth and saltines to pallid people in deck chairs, and if I tasted a cup now, the aroma blending with the salt air, I could probably remember the names of all the kids I prowled those great ships with more than forty years ago. Not many of the ships were American: they weren't popular with travelers because Prohibition was enforced and passengers could only drink in their cabins.

And it was still possible, as late as 1936, to work your way to California by signing on as a deck hand on a freighter. The journey took about six weeks, through the Panama Canal, with lots of stops en route. You were transported, fed, and paid—one cent. I tried it with a school friend the summer we were seventeen, and it has survived as a good memory, though not so much fun at the time.

Haven't you noticed that so many things, particularly those involving minor hardships, improve both with the telling and with the passage of years? In the case of our sea voyage, the union organizer aboard suggested we were no better than scabs and kept threatening various forms of mayhem as soon as we next got ashore; meanwhile, the third mate, a stout old salt who had gone up and down in the ranks like an elevator, was appalled by our sexual inexperience and vowed to arrange to get us laid at every stop. So we alternated between fear and hope at each port of call, and neither ever did come to pass. Both the National Maritime Union man and the third mate got drunk too soon to deliver on their promises.

There were no interstate highways when I explored America; you could really see the country close up. One summer, I drove a fifty dollar Model A Ford to California and back with a couple of college classmates. It took us several weeks. We slept in fields, curled up in blankets; we paused now and then to make gasoline money by picking peaches, or whatever, for a few cents an hour, and we enjoyed the hospitality that was lavished on us everywhere by strangers amazed to see New York license plates on a jalopy in, say, Elko, Nevada.

In west Texas, where we experienced our eighteenth flat tire of the journey, with a broken jack and no inner tubes, I hiked a mile to a lonely general store with our last twenty dollars in my jeans. An old man faced me across the counter, pointing a shotgun at my chest. He informed me I was in Texas, where people knocked before entering. Then I noticed the sign out front: William Attwood, Prop. I showed him my driving license. "Gawd awmighty, son!" he cried. "We are *cousins!*" Free meal, free gas, free inner tube. People were nice everywhere, not impersonal, like on the interstates.

Of course things were very different, as late as the sixties, if you were black. There were lynchings still when I was a kid. In South Carolina, where we were picking fruit, I went to get some water out of a drinking bucket. The foreman knocked the ladle out of my hand. "You crazy, boy? That's the nigger bucket!" Later, in 1946, working in Washington, I deplored but accepted, like everyone else, the segregation that existed in the nation's capital. Only in the fifties, when I started meeting blacks as a reporter, did I begin to identify with their anger and frustration. It's hard to believe today that in 1955 the black editor of the *Atlanta Daily World* and I could not eat in public together in his city except in the back room of a "Negro" restaurant.

No, everything wasn't better in the good old days. But a hell of a lot was. Food was. The sandwiches I ordered at night when working late on the paper at Princeton were—I can still recall to this day the taste of the melted cheese, tomatoes and bacon with Russian dressing in a toasted number four from Renwick's cafeteria. We were strangers to the lukewarm glop encased in two slabs of flannel that the fast food chains have imposed on the present generation.

Even wars, though dangerous, could be perceived as noble and necessary causes and not as lunatic nuclear nightmares. And we felt like the good guys. People at home cheered us on; people overseas welcomed us, for the most part, as liberators. We really believed, many of us, that a brave new world, with democracy triumphant, was in the making.

Mine was not a war I enjoyed. But I saw a few places where things were still . . . different: Cairo at night, silent except for the hoofbeats of the horse-drawn gharrys; then, at dawn, the cocks crowing all over the city, and then the mullahs chanting in the minarets. Waikiki, quiet and uncrowded before the coconut palms gave way to the high-rise hotels. And back home, my town, New Canaan, surrounded still by my boyhood woods and meadows not yet bulldozed for housing developments and condominiums.

There were fewer conveniences, like electronic gadgetry, when I was growing up, and therefore fewer things that broke down. (Those that did could usually be fixed instead of replaced.) We had an ice man who came in a horse-drawn wagon with big blocks of ice that we chipped at with a pick; in the sweltering summer of 1948, the city room of the *New York Herald Tribune* was cooled not by air conditioners but by ceiling fans that merely stirred the cigarette smoke. We were used to it. We just wiped off the sweat so it wouldn't blot the copy paper and repaired frequently to Bleeck's bar downstairs for cold beer.

So our generation is probably the last to have a simpler, more natural, uncomputerized world to remember and reminisce about. I think we had more fun; at least we agonized less about ourselves, swallowed fewer pills, and seldom consulted shrinks. Certainly we were more upbeat—more hopeful about what tomorrow would bring and more optimistic about the world in which we lived.

And this solid base of memories, dappled by sunshine and shadow—the shadow lightening as time passes—serves us well in middle age. So do the multitudes of people who have been performers in the private pageants of our lives, who have joined our good times and shared our bad; or changed, if only slightly, the course of our personal history. How would I ever forget Dudley Fitts, who goaded me into trying to write well at sixteen, or Herbert Fitzroy, who taught me the importance of constructive indignation at college, or Henry Hough and Dan Mich, two of the most sensitive and exacting editors of my trade? And there was a sixteen-year-old blonde bridesmaid I met at a wedding in Riverdale, New York, and caught up with in Italy some years later and proposed to one rainy night in London and married on a bright June morning in Paris.

Not all our memories are pleasant, though a helpful brain tends to eliminate the worst, as one might airbrush a photograph. For example, I can easily recall the amusing highlights of a motor trip through central Europe with our two children in 1962—the cable car ride up to the *Zugspitze* in Bavaria, Peter's excitement at finding a hidden microphone in our hotel room in Prague, a family picnic in a sunlit alpine meadow where nothing went wrong; but I can only dimly recall the storm and stress—the incessant quarreling in the back seat, the problem of finding lodging every evening, the broken fan belt, the slivovitz hangover, the heat and the fatigue.

Bad memories are as inevitable as cuts and bruises, but we can and should make an effort to minimize them, just as we should try to avoid entrapment, as I suggested earlier, in activities that we know are going to be boring or stressful. A trip to the Soviet Union with Sim, Jan, and Suzy could have been fun to look back on, even though nothing turned out exactly as planned, if my female companions had not been at war with each other much of the time. After Sim and Jan had to leave, Suzy and I went on to Lapland and we have some good memories of that.

At home, too, a weekend spoiled by family quarrels can never be redeemed, and there comes a time when you realize there are only fifty-two weekends a year, and the years are rushing by, and you just can't afford to spoil any more—not if you appreciate the value of storing up

good memories for the time ahead when that's all you'll
have left.

The storage process often takes some effort. When your
children are growing up, it's important to do things with
them (things *they* want to do) even if you might feel
more like spending time with your friends and contemporaries, playing adult games. When Peter was twelve,
I took him on a four-day canoe trip in Maine that lingers
in my memory as a nightmare of mosquito bites, sleepless
nights and aching muscles. But in retrospect I'm glad I
did, just as I'm glad I camped out with him and Jan in
an equatorial blizzard on Mount Kenya. (This was a considerably more rugged expedition than trudging up a
volcano with them and Sim in Guadaloupe, or touring
historic Williamsburg with Suzy). Shared memories, even
when they involve some discomfort, and even pain, are
the ties that bind families together long after the children
are grown and departed.

My best memories, the ones that give me that precious
solace mentioned in the last chapter, start with the summers of my tenth and eleventh birthdays, which I associate
with lots of friends, sunshine, salt water and mischief;
and proceed at intervals through the intervening decades
(how vividly I recall the first day I could lift my left arm
after a month of therapy at Bethesda Hospital!) up to the
present—to last evening, actually, when I heard my granddaughter, Marty, calling out at the beach picnic, "I want
grandpa to sit over here next to me!"

Most of the bad memories, when not airbrushed or
filtered out, are more accurately regrets: I regret it took
me so long to discover that girls didn't regard physical
contact as distasteful; I regret wanting too much to be
liked by people to tell certain ones to go to hell; to this
day I regret wasting so much time as a teenager (as who

doesn't) when I could have been praticing the piano or
any musical instrument, perfecting my tennis and golf,
learning languages or at the very least becoming a really
good dancer instead of—hanging around; I regret certain
minor but hard to forget incidents when I unintentionally
hurt someone's feelings. For example, while I was in a
Rome restaurant a long time ago with a young German
actress, a French woman writer I knew passed our table
and made a cruel, unwarranted remark—I suppose because
the girl was German. I let it pass; in retrospect, I shouldn't
have—there were tears in her eyes and venom in the
French woman's. By contrast, I don't regret reacting to an
offensive American expatriate in Paris who kept proclaiming at a party that Harry Truman, then our president,
was "a goddam communist"; my reaction was to suggest
he apologize and leave unless he wanted me to knock his
teeth through the back of his neck. He left quietly, and
I never did find out if that was a threat I could carry out;
but I've found it's one that usually works, since almost
everyone can be instantly subdued by a plausible threat of
physical violence. Be careful; I said *almost* everyone.

Regrets rise up from the depths on nights when you
can't get to sleep and then proceed to make sleep all but
impossible. They come in all sizes and models—insignif-
icant, routine/depressive, and recurring/traumatic. Coping with them is easier after you classify them. Some you
just know are going to haunt you forever, like destitute
in-laws, so you simply summon up the stoicism and reenact
the frustration—which sometimes dissipates it—and take
ten milligrams of Valium if all else fails.

There are two varieties of midlife regrets that serve
no purpose—none—and that must therefore be guarded

against. One can be labeled, "Why not?" and the other, "What if?"

My own examples of why nots (starting with neglected piano practice) are countless, although I have managed, mercifully, to forget a few. Why didn't I get off the night train at Katowice, in Poland, in 1947 with the lovely blonde who spoke French instead of dutifully going on to Wroclaw to interview the communist mayor? Why didn't I say yes to a job offer with *The New Yorker* in the fall of 1941 and become a war correspondent instead of staying in law school under parental pressure and then losing control of my life in the Rube Goldberg machinery of the United States Army? Why didn't Sim and I accept Ernest Hemingway's invitation to go deep-sea fishing in Cuba in 1957 instead of rushing back to New York to deliver copy personally to my editor? (I could have phoned it in.) And why, like every American my age, didn't I put every penny I saved into real estate back in the 1950s?

What ifs are even more insomnia-prolonging than why nots.

For example: What if, having just returned from Cuba and a long talk with Fidel Castro in July, 1959, I had discussed the trip and the conversation with Jack Kennedy? The opportunity knocked. The week I got back, I was staying with Ben Bradlee at his house on N Street in Georgetown, and Kennedy, who lived down the block, dropped in for a beer after dinner. We sat in the kitchen and talked about—I forget. Not Cuba. But had I been able to persuade him of what I knew, for instance, of the CIA's faulty intelligence estimates, of Castro's own uncertainties, of his widespread popular support—might not we have avoided the Bay of Pigs disaster nine months later, the subsequent frightening missile crisis—and all the rest? Perhaps. What *did* we talk about in the kitchen? Women, I guess.

And what if, when I was offered the ambassadorship to Guinea and was told by Pierre Salinger at the White House that the president had also approved me for Thailand or Morocco, I had said to hell with taking the kids to a hardship post; and then gone to where it was interesting but not so unhealthy that I contracted polio and my children had to be sent home?

What if I had stayed with Ultra in World War II— deciphering cables, briefing generals, rising in the ranks, seeing Europe in comfort, no mud on my boots—instead of stubbornly insisting on going to where the combat was? What if? Well, maybe I'd have been run over by a taxi coming out of a London night club in the blackout instead of escaping the grenade fragments that tore up my Canadian companion in Okinawa. You never know. So why brood over decisions that could turn out badly either way? My decisions, and I regret plenty of them, have at least allowed me the opportunity to ruminate about the alternatives many decades later.

You can conjecture endlessly and to no avail long into the night, knowing as we all do sooner or later that what might have been will never be—unless maybe you finally fall asleep and dream it in surrealistic spectacolor with a cast of thousands, all missing mythical planes and flunking imaginary exams.

And so regrets should be jettisoned—except for those that can teach us something—like detachment or forgiveness—and good memories should be preserved and cherished. For we are the sum total of our memories; to a considerable extent we have been formed by them, mellowed by them, inspired by them. Those of my contemporaries who say, "Forget the past," are doubly wrong

—not only because you can't help looking back at where you've been but because there's no way to slam the door on any part of your life, not without a lobotomy. By all means let's look ahead and make plans for next summer when we're sixty-two; but let's not hesitate to reminisce about the other summers we've known.

Some of these were good and some not so good, as is always the case in real life. So we try to keep adding more of those good and increasingly precious summers, and winters, one at a time, year in and year out, to our memory banks for quick reference. For this is when we can really savor them, even as we notice that the sun is going down.

15

CONTINUING

THERE HAVE BEEN a lot of references to twilight, dusk and darkening skies in this book—all metaphors for the irreversible aging process. One reason is that in middle age we begin to realize that sunset can last a long time; more and more people live on past seventy, past eighty and, like my mother, two aunts and an uncle, past ninety.

My own preference is for a quick sunset—the kind they have in the tropics, where daylight turns to nightfall as soon as the sun dips below the horizon. In terms of a life, it's like dying as Adlai Stevenson did, relatively young at sixty-five and very suddenly: no lingering twilight years of fading powers, memory loss and nursing care. My father, who died at 86, was headed that way after his last ill-

ness, but his doctor fortunately gave us the option of pro-
longing his half-life another few months with drugs, or
letting him pass on quietly and naturally. We chose the
humane and natural way.

Another reason for all the twilight talk is that, in middle
age, we become conscious not only of our approaching
mortality but of the imminent next phase of existence,
which is old age. While the only alternative to growing
old, as the saying goes, is dying young, a visit to a nursing
home, even an expensive one, can't help but make the
second alternative seem more attractive than it sounds.

When does old age start; or, to put it another way, when
does middle age end?

Earlier, I suggested that middle age usually starts with
an eye-opening event, like my talk with the young woman
in Nairobi; but that it needn't end until you think of
yourself as old, when others, sensing it, then perceive you
as such. But there are also certain symptoms which can't
be disregarded. Progressive deafness, a gradual diminution
of energy, chronic ill-health—all these hasten the transition
from middle to old. And there's a chronological factor,
especially if you're a woman. For example, I've known
active men in their seventies who are still thought of as
"middle aged" by their younger associates; but it's difficult
for me to regard a woman who admits to seventy—never
mind the face lifts and other shoring up—as being anything
but old.

Nowhere, in my experience, is the aging process more
dramatically visible than on the first Saturday of June at
Princeton University. That's when successive reunion
classes, starting with the oldest and spanning nearly eighty
years of undergraduate life, march in a two-mile long
procession from Nassau Hall across the campus to the
baseball field. The tradition originated in 1895, when the

older alumni got tired of having the younger and more nimble graduates beat them to the best seats at the game. So a procession was arranged, dubbed the P-rade, with the classes in chronological order and the last year's graduates bringing up the rear.

What makes the event dramatic and, to many spectators, emotionally unsettling is that you are watching the actual infirmities and ravages of age passing by, in reverse order. And at any point in the march past you can see yourself as you looked five, ten, fifteen or more years ago—and, worse, how you'll probably look in the years you may have left.

The start is sedate, once the lead-off twenty-fifth reunion "honor class" is out of the way. The first classes in line—with two or five or seven survivors—ride in golf carts driven by undergraduates. Then come younger but depleted contingents moving slowly with canes, smiling, most of them, but some a little vacantly.

By the time the Class of 1920 appears—these are men in their early eighties—there are a few walking erect and almost briskly. And with every later class, 1925, 1927, there are more alumni smiling and waving to the crowd. But there's no mistaking them as anything but . . . old.

The big change, from old to middle-aged, is evident now in the classes of the mid-thirties: these are men for the most part not yet seventy, and you can spot a few heads not wholly white or bald. My own class, 1941, is a mixture —some of us look like the younger brothers of others, and we still have the energy to pause and give football cheers to the younger classes lining the route, cheers that are then returned.

The last P-rade I went to, in 1981, was the first which I watched with an eye to delineating the line between middle and old age. And I concluded that it happens for most men somewhere between the forty-fifth and fifty-second reunion classes—that is, at some point between sixty-seven and seventy-four. And that's what makes the sixties such an important decade in anyone's life: It's the last really active one. Later on, you can cling to bits of authority and activity and show up at meetings and be treated with courtesy and even deference—but you just aren't considered a participant in much of anything. And after seventy-five, to quote an Alan King gag, all a man wants to hear are two things: "Who's your tailor?" and "Stay away from my broad."

There are exceptions, of course, and not only in the Soviet Politburo. Among those I've known personally who remained as vibrant and contemporary after seventy as before have been Averell Harriman, Walter Lippmann, Chou En Lai, Barbara Tuchman, Maurice Chevalier, Coco Chanel, Robert Moses, Bricktop, Groucho Marx—and my parents. And although I never met them, I'm sure Picasso, Bertrand Russell and George Burns are others whose lives have proved that vitality *can* persist long past three score and ten.

Looking back, during that Princeton weekend, I reflected that I'd come here as an undergraduate in the second decade of my life and had come now, as an alumnus, in my seventh. And I concluded that every one of the intervening decades has been, all things considered, an improvement over the preceding one. And no, I don't think this makes me so very exceptional.

We all know that the teens, beset by self-consciousness and insecurities, are overrated. But the struggling twenties and thirties, the decades of child rearing and job mobility, carry their own excess baggage of anxieties and compulsions. Most people start shucking off some of these useless burdens in their forties, but their careers are usually cresting then, and some are wondering if they're in the right one. It isn't really until the fifties, at least in my case, that the serenity that comes with self-confidence and self-knowledge begins to penetrate your psyche. You make fewer mistakes and fewer bad judgments about people. You finally apply some of the lessons you've learned over the years the hard way. You expect less and achieve more. You begin to comprehend the nature of love.

And the sixties, if your health holds up, can be even more relaxing and rewarding. Routine work tapers off, but purposeful or creative activity may burgeon. Neurotic constraints and inhibitions tend to evaporate, along with the compulsion to conform. (Not for everybody, of course: I remember watching a television news show recently where Mrs. Reagan, on her sixtieth birthday, felt obliged to declare she was really fifty-eight; and in the commercial that followed, Pete Rose, the ball player, said he used Grecian Formula to avoid gray hair and the awful possibility that his teammates might start calling him "old-timer.")

What also makes the sixties invigorating is that these years can be a time of maximum freedom of expression and minimum conformity to convention. Of course you have to make an effort; the behavioral patterns of a lifetime are a lot harder to change than a pair of shoes, even when you can feel them pinching.

But if I can feel good about the sixties, don't expect me to recommend the seventies. I won't get there for a while yet, but there's no way—no way—I can conceive of that decade as being an improvement over this one. Already, lots of things are getting harder to do. Sex comes to mind, naturally. And hearing, especially if there's background noise, becomes a challenge. Stairs seem steeper and suitcases heavier, while drinking slightly more than your accustomed ration before dinner (or anything at all after dinner) produces such woeful and interminable hangovers that some genial habits of a lifetime have to be discarded. If you read *The New Yorker,* you begin to notice that almost none of the celebrities mentioned in the magazine's annual Christmas greeting poem are familiar; there was a time when they all were. A theme song for the years after sixty could well be entitled "So many memories, so little memory." My mother remembers very little about yesterday and her plans for tomorrow but a great deal about her visit to St. Petersburg, Russia, in 1906. I am just now beginning to appreciate her problem. The other day, the phone rang in my bedroom. It was an old friend from State Department days. "You know," I said, "when you called I was trying to remember why I'd come into the bedroom. Now I know why. It was to look for my glasses, which I was actually wearing."

"That's nothing," he said. "I'm on the second floor. Halfway up the stairs, I couldn't remember whether I was going up or down."

At the Century, an old and venerated New York club I belong to, a Century martini is a euphemism for a double: order one and they bring you two in a small pewter jug. One day, it is said, an old and distinguished member, gesturing vainly to a new waiter for a *second* Century, finally caught the man's attention. "Do you know who I am?" he demanded sharply.

"No, sir," replied the waiter, "but I'll make inquiries and let you know."

And they tell of the two ancient members who met by chance in the lobby. "Harry!" exclaimed one. "How nice to see you! I thought we were *both* dead!"

I really don't care to keep going that long.

As it is, I feel estranged from the millions of my fellow

Americans who buy the supermarket weeklies to read about the newest instant cure for arthritis, the latest UFO invasion, the astrological forecasts, the eat-all-you-want diets, and the alleged sexual aberrations of entertainers I've never heard of; estranged, too, from the bushy-tailed young men wooed by *Oui,* which, raunch-wise, is supposedly about one f-stop past *Penthouse* and whose editorial philosophy is advertised as, "We will help you reach your dreams."

And, to tell the truth, I don't particularly want to see the twenty-first century. I can't perceive any dramatic progress in the offing, except in technology, and computers aren't my bag. Also I think a number of nuclear disasters are likely, given the pace of proliferation. Yet only destruction and casualties on a large scale will bring home to the human race, once and for all, the criminal folly of even making plans for a war with nuclear weapons. Meanwhile we will continue to live in mortal danger, something many of us have grown tired of repeating to people unable to grasp how drastically the world has changed since Hiroshima. (I can still recall the lead of my first front page by-lined story in the New York *Herald Tribune*—back in March, 1946: "The blunt fact that mankind faces self-destruction unless the United Nations control atomic power was made very plain in a seventy-seven page report issued today. . . ." That was the so-called Acheson-Baruch-Lilienthal report, and when the Russians rejected it, the cold war was launched.)

Right now I'd say the odds on our keeping the planet habitable into the next century are only slightly better than even, not good enough to make me yearn for longevity.

And I suspect the things people do will continue to be less fun with each passing year, in part because of a more cramped and harried environment, in part because of violence bred by frustration and in part because wonder and adventure are in abeyance. There will be fewer surprises in store, and less to marvel at. The moon, we've seen, is just a heap of lifeless rocks, and there are no Martians after all. Not long ago, an elderly lady was telling one of my friends, a book reviewer, why she hadn't been shocked by a recent steamy novel: "You see, my dear, fuck doesn't mean what it used to."

Meanwhile, what's the indicated activity for us as the shadows lengthen on the lawn? I sometimes reflect on the four key words I cited in the first chapter—love, courage, integrity and humor—and when I measure my life today against these bench marks, I come out feeling pretty good about where I am. I love and am loved, though a stranger observing me in the company of my nearest and dearest relatives might at times be unconvinced. Love manifests itself in many different ways.

Courage? Well, you feel it inside you or you don't, and it's not that often you get a chance to demonstrate it, physical courage especially. I know I can handle the scary hospital stuff but I've yet to find out how I'd acquit myself with a mugger; cravenly, I think. I would just like to qualify for membership in the aristocracy that the novelist E. M. Forster described in 1939 in these words: "I believe in an aristocracy—if that is the right word, and if a democrat may use it. Not an aristocracy of power, based upon rank and influence, but an aristocracy of the sensitive, the considerate and the plucky. Its members are to be found in all nations and classes, and all through the ages, and there is a secret understanding between them when they meet. They represent the true human tradition, the one permanent victory of our queer race over cruelty and chaos." Plucky is a good word.

Integrity is ingrained early in life, and part of the pleasure of aging is that you can be more positive and outspoken about what you know, from experience and intuition, to be the truth. Getting at the truth of things—distilling out the flimflam—is a worthy endeavor at any age but can become an absorbing occupation in your later years, especially when bullshit is piling up worldwide faster than municipal garbage. Just remember Emerson's admonition that we are given a choice between truth and repose but cannot have both. And bear in mind something Walter Lippmann wrote in 1960, at the close of the slack Eisenhower years: "Why is it bad to shrug off the ideal standards of honesty in politics, business and love? Because it defeats us and frustrates our lives. . . . We are very rich, but we are not having a very good time. For our life, though it is full of things, is empty of the kind of purpose and effort that gives to life its flavor and its meaning."

Humor, always important to me, has become practically essential in my late middle age. It's what cushions, eases, enlivens and illuminates life at a certain point in time, as well as being a sanity preserver (and in Norman Cousins' case, a lifesaver). For example, I've collected jokes for about forty years—not one-liners but stories that build slowly to a climax, with the humor contained as much in the situation and the telling as in the punch line. And fun, for me, has always been performing one of these stories to a congenial group of friends.

So my agenda for the rest of my sixties will surely include as much expressed love and life-sustaining laughter and prospecting for truth as I can fit in, along with some writing and travel, and some learning of new skills and,

who knows, perhaps something unexpected. In "Ulysses,"
Tennyson wrote:

> *Old age hath yet his honor and his toil.*
> *Death closes all; but something ere the end,*
> *Some work of noble note, may yet be done* . . .

So I'm open to suggestion; which makes me feel . . .
almost young.

And in our sixties the burden of anxieties and obligations that was strapped on our backs for so long can finally
be laid down. I do, though, feel an obligation to tidy up
some of the litter of my life: there are papers, memos,
letters, and documents filed away in my back room at
home that might just be of some use to a young twenty-
first century scholar doing a thesis, say, on why *Collier's*
folded with a circulation of more than 3 million in 1956.
So I owe it to him or her to assemble the material they'll
need and take it for safekeeping and storage to Wisconsin,
where the State Historical Society maintains a mass communications center full of similar archives. Otherwise the
leftover records of a lifetime will get tossed out. For myself, this bothers me not at all: obits are of interest only
to survivors who need evidence they had a moderately
prominent relative, and memorabilia are of interest only
to survivors who figure there might be a valuable autograph or letter among them. But helping out future students of some aspect of history that I was involved in does
make it worthwhile to me to sort out my papers this
winter and turn them over to Wisconsin.

My agenda will also include paying more attention to
what a scientist like Edward O. Wilson has identified as
"our most intense emotions." He listed these as "enthu-

siasm and a sharpening of the senses from exploration; exaltation from discovery; triumph in battle and competitive sports; the restful satisfaction from an altruistic act well and truly placed; the stirring of ethnic and national pride; the strength from family ties; and the secure biophilic pleasure from the nearness of animals and growing plants."

Exploration and discovery—by all means. Triumph— well, I do beat Sim and Suzy at croquet occasionally. Altruistic acts—sure. Ethnic and national pride—we Wasps don't flaunt the ethnic thing, but I would like to feel more patriotic pride in the actions of my country than I have in recent years; perhaps I will if this administration begins to see the world clearly, as it really is, and not through clouded academic and ideological lenses. (As I write this, there is not much evidence that it has, or will.) Family ties—well, we're all in touch, within reach, and on pretty good terms: more is too much to expect. As for being close to plants and animals, I plan to avoid cities as much as possible, where the plants are in pots and the animals on leashes or in cages.

I also plan to enjoy the feeling of cool ocean water on my skin as often as I can manage it. At every onset of melancholy, I plan to take inventory of my accomplishments and future opportunities, which quite often helps. When it appears my time is up, I expect to get in line without panic, expecting neither reward nor punishment for how I put my years on earth to use.

There are some old late-evening activities I'll no longer indulge in, like getting into heated but futile political arguments. I've had strong feelings about our hidebound and unimaginative foreign and domestic policies for years, but since I'm no longer in a position to exert any appreciable influence on them, I confine my comments to an occasional short piece of writing or a straight answer when asked a question.

Now and then I do go to a meeting and say something certain to create a few waves that at least interrupt the boredom, something for which the audience is invariably grateful. Not long ago, at a Council on Foreign Relations convocation to discuss yet another report on South Africa, I made the point that exactly twenty years before, in Lagos, I had helped draft a similar report for a conference of United States ambassadors; it struck me that the recommendations were almost identical, even though the effect of the 1961 document on the status of civil and human rights in South Africa had been imperceptible. Apartheid was still firmly entrenched, and the Afrikaaner power structure as intransigent. Would there be still another report issued twenty years from now? What would it say? And did we really think, I asked, that history would oblige us by marking time? That sort of meeting is worth attending.

But I'm beginning to stray from the subject of this book, so I'll check my impulse to say a few things about the spent force of communism or the trouble Americans have in putting themselves in other people's shoes.

Having by now made it through much of middle age, I find myself in the same place before the same typewriter nearly a year after writing word one of this essay. And not too much has changed in a year. A new puppy is nibbling on my bare toe; the roof of a newly-built barn intrudes on my view, but the way our hemlocks are growing, the roof should be nicely screened out two summers from now. Looking at the trees reminds me of E. B.

White's short story, "The Second Tree from the Corner," which I reread the other night after Suzy brought the book containing it home from the library. And in the restless contentment that best describes my mood these days, I felt a certain kinship with Trexler, White's middle-aged protagonist, as he stood on the sidewalk outside his psychiatrist's office:

> Trexler found himself renewed by the remembrance that what he wanted was at once great and microscopic, and that although it borrowed from the nature of large deeds and of youthful love and of old songs and early intimations, it was not any one of these things, and that it had not been isolated or pinned down, and that a man who attempted to define it in the privacy of a doctor's office would fall flat on his face.

One editor, after reading a part of my manuscript, said he found it "strangely depressing." Well, of course he did. This book is about life—mine, for the most part—and life is by no means a bowl of cherries nor a glorious cycle of song; in fact, it can often be very depressing indeed. And it can defeat you unless you develop what F. Scott Fitzgerald called "the wise and tragic sense of life." In other words, unless you grow up.

That's what makes this final full decade of active middle age so much better than it promised to be a few years back. For by the time you reach sixty, you generally have matured at least enough to accept life as it is. You even learn to appreciate unexpected small surprises, such as the letter—not a phone call but an actual letter—I received from my daughter Jan yesterday.

And you should by now have some idea of what living is all about. A while back, I read a piece in the *New York*

Times by a teacher who said a "troubled" young girl had asked him what he thought the purpose of life was. "To figure out whether God exists or not," he told her. What nonsense to impart to a troubled teenager—or anyone else. How can you "figure out" that answer? In a lab? On a blackboard? By revelation, perhaps, but does that prove God exists or only that your need for God is so desperate that you will create such a supreme being in your own mind? I think you can louse up a lot of leisure time getting engaged in such a quixotic enterprise.

I prefer my own already stated definition of life's purpose—to enjoy it. And I agree with James Michener, who said, "In the hereafter, each man will be asked to explain why he abstained from those normal pleasures to which he was entitled." I would only alter it to read, "to which he or she was entitled." No God I could conceive of would object to our enjoying the time placed at our disposal.

In a moment, my particular enjoyment will be to commemorate these final sentences of what has not at times been an easy book to write by having a cold beer, and quite possibly another, while I begin to ponder some projects to undertake in the coming winter months. I like projects. And what the hell, I'm only sixty-two. I don't want to stop moving. Not until I have to. Because I've known people who did, and they got old real fast.

Born in Paris sixty-two years ago, William Attwood has been a journalist for most of his working life, except for four years in the army and five as a United States ambassador in Africa.

As a veteran of thirty-one years of marriage and the father of three children, Attwood gets his enjoyment mainly from his two grandchildren, sports—like tennis and swimming, which have helped him recover from polio and two heart attacks—the company of old friends, and visiting out-of-the-way places with his wife, Sim.

Attwood, who retired at sixty as president and publisher of *Newsday,* keeps busy teaching, writing, lecturing, and serving on his town's legislative council as well as on national committees he considers worthwhile—but all at his own pace. "I used to be in the rat race," he says, "until I realized that even if I won, I'd still be a rat."